THE KEY

STUDENT STUDY GUIDE

THE KEY

THE KEY series of student study guides is specifically designed to assist students in preparing for unit tests, final exams, and provincial examinations. Each **KEY** includes questions, answers, detailed solutions, and practice tests. The complete solutions show problem-solving methods, explain key concepts, and highlight potential errors.

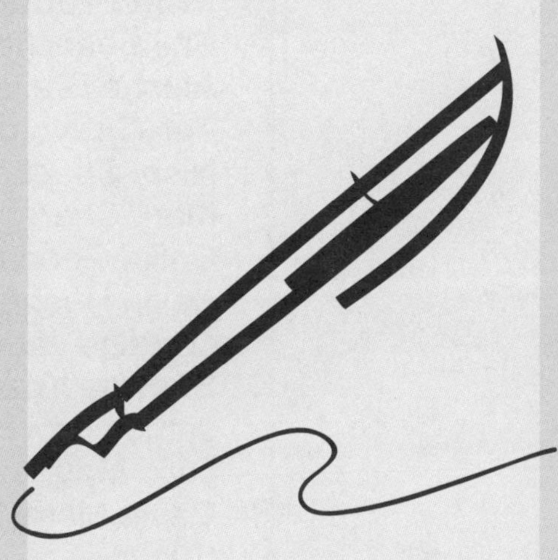

Reading

Listening

Viewing

Writing

Speaking

Representing

B.C. Edition

Canadian Cataloguing in Publication Data

Rao, Gautam, 1961 –
THE KEY – English 10 (B.C.)

1.   English – Juvenile Literature. I. Title

Published by
Castle Rock Research Corp.
2340 Manulife Place
10180 – 101 Street
Edmonton, AB T5J 3S4

5 6 7 FP 07 06 05

Printed in Canada

Publisher:
Gautam Rao

Editors:
Mun Prasad
Shirley Wacowich

Contributor:
Jodi MacQuarrie

Print Production:
Phil Beauchamp
Alesha Braitenbach
Tory Braybrook
Nishi Chadha
Mark Chan
Collin Goodman
Kevin Huenison
Lorraine James
Shawna Kozel
James Kropfreiter
Julie May
David Moret
Suzanne Morin
Jackie Pacheco
Tara Pratt
Abhinav Rastogi
Diana Seguin
Jan Witwicky
Gary Yaremchuk
Richard Yeomans

Dedicated to the memory of Dr. V. S. Rao

THE KEY for English 10 is specifically designed with students' needs in mind. The first part of *THE KEY* introduces students to the different genres that comprise the English 10 curriculum. The second part of the guide has been created with the English 10 Foundation Skills Assessment (FSA) in mind. Working through practice questions that are modeled after provincial examination questions will help to familiarize students with the types of questions that are typically used. The following is a summary of the main sections of *THE KEY.*

Key Factors Contributing to School Success provides students with examples of study and review strategies. Topics include information on learning styles, study schedules, and developing review notes.

Part A – Reading and Writing

This section examines the different genres and includes tips on how to write effectively. Part A begins with a discussion of how various genres are defined. The discussion of the short story contains an introduction to literary topics such as plot and characterization. The unit on poetry reviews some fundamentals of the poetic text, including meter and rhyme. Within each section, sample readings help to reinforce the process of creating meaning from text. The media communications section highlights some important elements to keep in mind while viewing graphics, cartoons, and movies. Within each section, students have an opportunity to work on sample questions testing their understanding of the genres reviewed.

Key Strategies for Success on Exams explores topics such as common exam question formats and strategies for responding, directing words most commonly used, how to begin the exam, and managing test anxiety.

Part B – Practice Examinations

This section includes three multiple choice practice examinations that reflect the multiple choice questions on the English 10 Foundation Skills Assessment. Questions on these exams have been carefully constructed to correspond to the FSA and include detailed solutions that fully explain each answer.

THE KEY *Study Guides* are available for Principles of Mathematics 10, English 10, and Science 10. A complete list of ***THE KEY*** Study Guides available for grades 4-12 is included at the back of this book.

For information about any of our resources or services, please call Castle Rock Research at 250.868.8384 or visit our web site at http://www.castlerockresearch.com.

At Castle Rock Research we strive to produce a resource that is error-free. If you should find an error, please contact us so that future editions can be corrected.

CONTENTS

NOTES

KEY FACTORS CONTRIBUTING TO SCHOOL SUCCESS

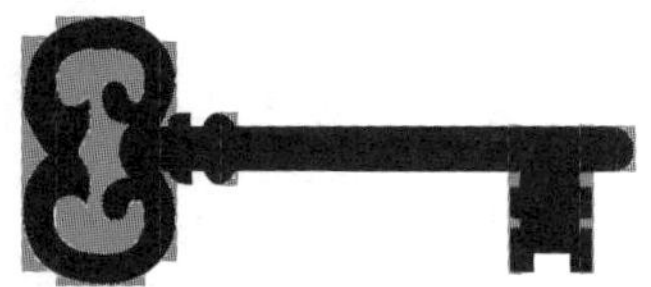

KEY FACTORS CONTRIBUTING TO SCHOOL SUCCESS

You want to do well in school. There are many factors that contribute to your success. While you may not have control over the number or types of assignments and tests that you need to complete, there are many factors that you can control to improve your academic success in any subject area. The following are examples of these factors.

- **REGULAR CLASS ATTENDANCE** – helps you to master the subject content, identify key concepts, take notes and receive important handouts, ask your teacher questions, clarify information, use school resources, and meet students with whom you can study

- **POSITIVE ATTITUDE AND PERSONAL DISCIPLINE** – helps you to come to classes on time, prepared to work and learn, complete all assignments to the best of your ability, and contribute to a positive learning environment

- **SELF-MOTIVATION AND PERSONAL DISCIPLINE** – helps you to set personal learning goals, take small steps continually moving toward achieving your goals, and to "stick it out when the going gets tough"

- **ACCESSING ASSISTANCE WHEN YOU NEED IT** – helps you to improve or clarify your understanding of the concept or new learning before moving on to the next phase

- **MANAGING YOUR TIME EFFICIENTLY** – helps you to reduce anxiety and focus your study and review efforts on the most important concepts

- **DEVELOPING 'TEST WISENESS'** – helps to increase your confidence in writing exams if you are familiar with the typical exam format, common errors to avoid, and know how the concepts in a subject area are usually tested

- **KNOWING YOUR PERSONAL LEARNING STYLE** – helps you to maximize your learning by using effective study techniques, developing meaningful study notes, and make the most efficient use of your study time

📖 KNOW YOUR LEARNING STYLE

You have a unique learning style. Knowing your learning style – how you learn best – can help you to maximize your time in class and during your exam preparation. There are seven common learning styles. Read the following descriptions to see which one most closely describes your learning preferences.

- **LINGUISTIC LEARNER** (sometimes referred to as an auditory learner) – learns best by saying, hearing and seeing words; is good at memorizing things such as dates, places, names and facts

- **LOGICAL/MATHEMATICAL LEARNER** – learns best by categorizing, classifying and working with abstract relationships; is good at mathematics, problem solving and reasoning

- **SPATIAL LEARNER** (sometimes referred to as a visual learner) – learns best by visualizing, seeing, working with pictures; is good at puzzles, imaging things, and reading maps and charts

- **MUSICAL LEARNER** – learns best by hearing, rhythm, melody, and music; is good at remembering tones, rhythms and melodies, picking up sounds

- **BODILY/KINESTHETIC LEARNER** – learns best by touching, moving, and processing knowledge through bodily sensations; is good at physical activities

- **INTERPERSONAL LEARNER** – learns best by sharing, comparing, relating, cooperating; is good at organizing, communicating, leading, and understanding others

- **INTRAPERSONAL LEARNER** – learns best by working alone, individualized projects, and self-paced instruction

(Adapted from http://snow.utoronto.ca/Learn2/mod3/mlstyles.html)

Your learning style may not fit "cleanly" into one specific category but may be a combination of two or more styles. Knowing your personal learning style allows you to organize your study notes in a manner that provides you with the most meaning. For example, if you are a spatial or visual learner, you may find mind mapping and webbing are effective ways to organize subject concepts, information, and study notes. If you are a linguistic learner, you may need to write and then "say out loud" the steps in a process, the formula, or actions that lead up to a significant event. If you are a kinesthetic learner you may need to use your finger to trace over a diagram to remember it or to "tap out" the steps in solving a problem or "feel" yourself writing or typing the formula.

📖 SCHEDULING STUDY TIME

Effective time management skills are an essential component to your academic success. The more effectively you manage your time the more likely you are to achieve your goals such as completing all of your assignments on time or finishing all of the questions on a unit test or year-end exam. Developing a study schedule helps to ensure you have adequate time to review the subject content and prepare for the exam.

You should review your class notes regularly to ensure you have a clear understanding of the new material. Reviewing your lessons on a regular basis helps you to learn and remember the ideas and concepts. It also reduces the quantity of material that you must study prior to a unit test or year-end exam. If this practice is not part of your study habits, establishing a study schedule will help you to make the best use of your time. The following are brief descriptions of three types of study schedules.

- **LONG-TERM STUDY SCHEDULE** – begins early in the school year or semester and well in advance of an exam; is the **most effective** manner for improving your understanding and retention of the concepts, and increasing self-confidence; involves regular, nightly review of class notes, handouts and text material

- **SHORT-TERM STUDY SCHEDULE** – begins **five to seven days prior to an exam**; must organize the volume of material to be covered beginning with the most difficult concepts; each study session starts with a brief review of what was studied the day before

- **CRAMMING** – occurs the night before an exam; is the **least effective** form of studying or exam preparation; focuses on memorizing and reviewing critical information such as facts, dates, formulas; do not introduce new material; has the potential to increase exam anxiety by discovering something you do not know

Regardless of the type of study schedule you use, you may want to consider the following to maximize your study time and effort:

- establish a regular time and place for doing your studying

- minimize distractions and interruptions during your study time

- plan a ten minute break for every hour that you study

- organize the material so you begin with the most challenging content first

- divide the subject content into smaller manageable "chunks" to review

- develop a marking system for your study notes to identify key and secondary concepts, concepts that you are confident about, those that require additional attention or about which you have questions

- reward yourself for sticking to your schedule and/or completing each review section

- alternate the subjects and type of study activities to maintain your interest and motivation

- make a daily task list with the headings "must do", "should do", and "could do"

- begin each session by quickly reviewing what you studied the day before

- maintain your usual routine of eating, sleeping, and exercising to help you concentrate for extended periods of time

📖 *KEY* STRATEGIES FOR REVIEWING

Reviewing textbook material, class notes, and handouts should be an ongoing activity and becomes more critical in preparing for exams. You may find some of the following strategies useful in completing your review during your scheduled study time.

READING OR SKIMMING FOR KEY INFORMATION

- Before reading the chapter, preview it by noting headings, charts and graphs, chapter questions.

- Turn each heading and sub-heading into a question before you start to read.

- Read the complete introduction to identify the key information that is addressed in the chapter.

- Read the first sentence of the next paragraph for the main idea.

- Skim the paragraph noting key words, phrases, and information.

- Read the last sentence of the paragraph.

- Repeat the process for each paragraph and section until you have skimmed the entire chapter.

- Read the complete conclusion to summarize each chapter's contents.

- Answer the questions you created.

- Answer the chapter questions.

CREATING STUDY NOTES

Mind Mapping or Webbing

- Use the key words, ideas or concepts from your reading or class notes to create a *mind map or web* (a diagram or visual representation of the information). A mind map or web is sometimes referred to as a knowledge map.

- Write the key word, concept, theory or formula in the centre of your page.

- Write and link related facts, ideas, events, and information to the central concept using lines.

- Use colored markers, underlining, or other symbols to emphasize things such as relationships, information of primary and secondary importance.

- The following example of a mind map or web illustrates how this technique can be used to develop an essay.

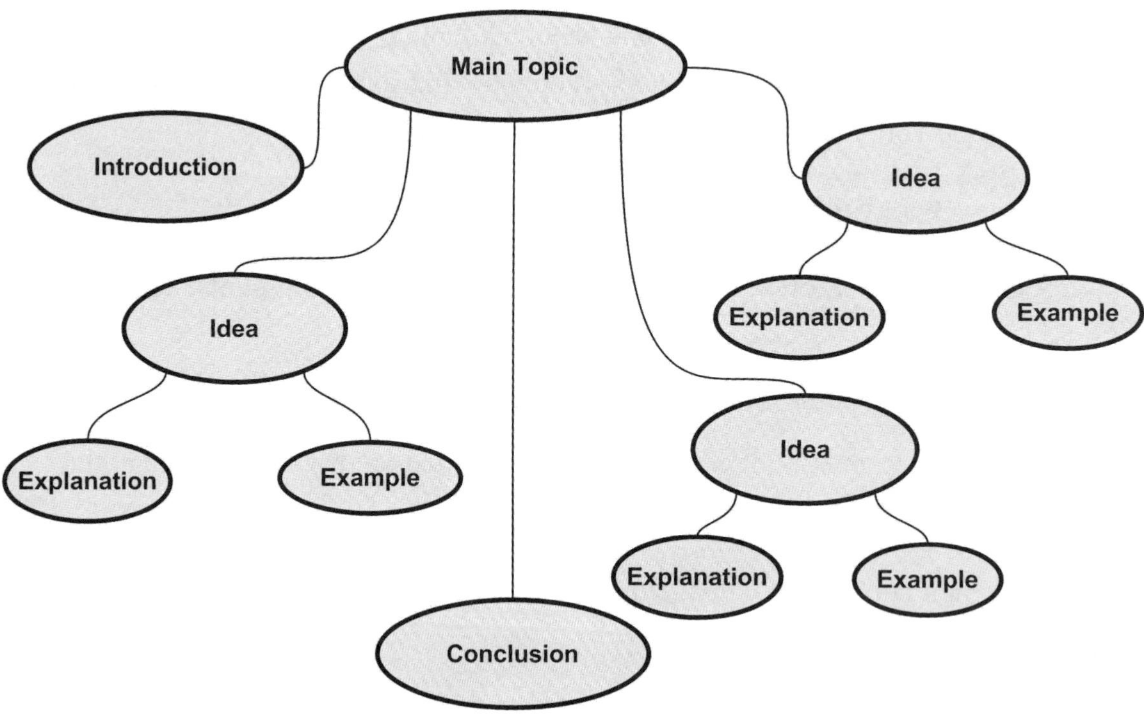

Charts

- ◆ Use charts to organize your information and relate theories, concepts, definitions, applications and other important details.
- ◆ Collect and enter the information in key categories.
- ◆ Use the completed chart as a composite picture of the concept or information.

The following is an example of how a chart can be used to help you organize information when exploring an issue in subjects such as Social Studies, the Sciences, or Humanities.

Define Key Words		
1.		
2.		
3.		
Explore the Issue		
Yes to the Issue	**No** to the Issue	**Maybe** to the Issue
1.	1.	1.
2.	2.	2.
3.	3.	3.
Case Studies and **Examples**		
1.	1.	
2.	2.	
3.	3.	
Defense of Your Point of View		
1.		
2.		
3.		

Index Cards

- Write a key event, fact, concept, theory, word or question on one side of the index card.
- On the reverse side, write the date, place, important actions and key individuals involved in the event, significance of the fact, salient features of the concept, essence and application of the theory, definition of the word or answer to the question.
- Use the cards to quickly review important information.

International System of Units (SI)

International System of Units (SI)

SI base unit

Base quantity	Name	Symbol
length	metre	m
mass	kilogram	kg
time	second	s
amount of substance	mole	mol

SI Prefixes

Factor	Name	Symbol
10^6	mega	M
10^3	kilo	k
10^{-2}	centi	c
10^{-3}	milli	m
10^{-6}	micro	μ

Derived Measures

Measures	Unit	Symbol
Volume	cubic metre	m^3

Symbols

- Develop your own symbols to use when reviewing your material to identify information you need in preparing for your exam. For example, an exclamation mark (!) may signify something that "must be learned well" because it is a key concept that is likely to appear on unit tests and the year-end exam. A question mark (?) may identify something you are unsure of while a star or asterisk (*) may identify important information for formulating an argument. A check mark (✓) or an (×) can be used to show that you agree or disagree with the statement, sentence or paragraph.

Crib Notes

- Develop brief notes that are a critical summary of the essential concepts, dates, events, theories, formulas, supporting facts, or steps in a process that are most likely to be on the exam.

- Use your crib notes as your "last minute" review before you go in to write your exam. You can not take crib notes into an exam.

MEMORIZING

- **ASSOCIATION** relates the new learning to something you already know. For example, in distinguishing between the spelling of 'dessert' and 'desert', you know 'sand' has only one 's' and so should desert.

- **MNEMONIC DEVICES** are sentences you create to remember a list or group of items. For example, the first letters of the words in the sentence "**E**very **G**ood **B**oy **D**eserves **F**udge" helps you to remember the names of the lines on the treble clef staff (E, G, B, D, and F) in music.

- **ACRONYMS** are words formed from the first letters of the words in a group. For example, **HOMES** helps you to remember the names of Canada's five Great Lakes (**H**uron, **O**ntario, **M**ichigan, **E**rie, and **S**uperior).

- **VISUALIZING** requires you to use your mind's eye to "see" the chart, list, map, diagram, or sentence as it exists in your textbook, notes, on the board, computer screen or in the display.

NOTES

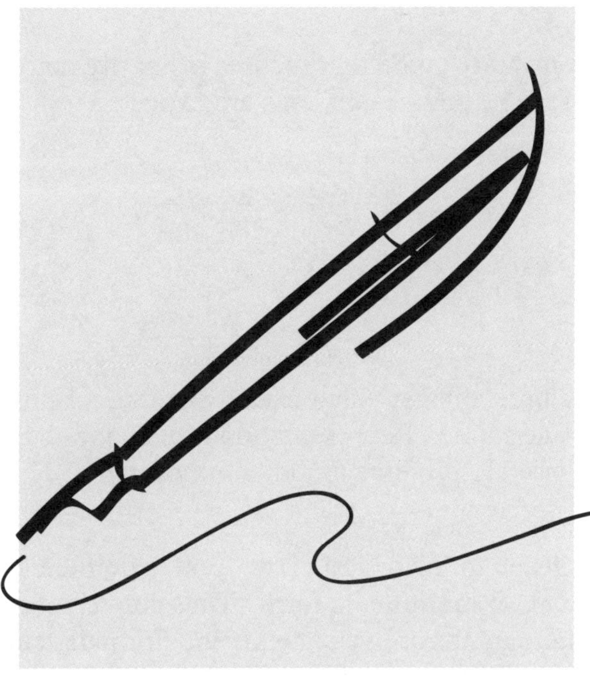

ENGLISH 10

PART A: READING AND WRITING

The Key for English 10 is a student study guide that focuses primarily on reading and writing. To meet the curriculum outcomes of the course, students are expected to:

- listen and speak
- read and write
- view and represent

Definitions

Representation is defined as a picture, collage, video, chart, diagram, or poster and certain kinds of performance such as tableaux and mime. Representation is also defined as including music and tone of voice when these are used to produce mood or atmosphere. This production is called text creation.

Texts are the things that students listen to, read, and view. Text is defined as any kind of communication in oral, print, visual, or multimedia form. Thus conversation is oral text, words written on paper are print text, photographs are visual text, and drum dancing and cartoon strips are examples of multimedia text. Authors, playwrights, photographers, cartoonists, and choreographers are all text creators.

This definition is not the common definition. Most people understand text to mean words written on a page. For example, your science book contains both text and illustrations, and most people think of theses as two different things but using the above definition, they are both text. This is a specialized meaning of the term of which students should be aware.

Context is perhaps a more familiar term. It has two closely related meanings. In a sentence, all the words before and after a particular word are the word's context. The context helps to explain the word's meaning. The same is true of all the words before or after a phrase, a paragraph, or an entire chapter.

Here is a stage direction from Romeo and Juliet.

> *Enter an officer, and three or four Citizens with clubs or **partisans***.

What is a *partisan*? The other word in the same context is clubs. The context makes it clear that clubs will do as well as partisans. Students can safely guess that a partisan is a weapon.

Context can also mean the entire situation in which something exists. This kind of context also helps to explain meaning. Everything that happens has a context.

> *The destruction of the World Trade Centre towers on September 11, 2001 must be understood in the context of world history.*

Texts also have context. A text is produced in a certain time and place and for a particular reason. Knowing the context may help the reader the viewer or the listener to better understand the situation as in the following examples and explanation.

> *In 1816, Mary Shelley had a nightmare vision of a young student constructing a monster. The nightmare led to her writing Frankenstein. The fact that she had the nightmare had a context: she and her companions had been telling ghost and horror stories for days. The content of her nightmare also had a context: Mary Shelley lived in a time of rapid change, when scientific advances were making many people uneasy. Widespread doubts about the reckless pursuit of knowledge help to explain the things she saw in her vision.*

Form and Genre

Genre sometimes means any classification of texts by form, style, or subject matter. However, a more careful definition distinguishes between form and genre.

☞ **Form describes structure.**

Examples of Forms	Characteristics
Letter	Generally begins with an inside address and date; uses conventional greeting and closings like 'Dear— ' and 'Yours Sincerely'
Memorandum	Often brief and addressed to a limited group such as the employees of a company; limited to essential information
Short story	20,000 words or less; usually few characters, one main character; a single plot
Novel	Over 50,000 words; usually 90,000 to 100,000 or more; may contain many characters and multiple plots within the main story
Novella	20,000 to 50,000 words; a shorter version of a novel
Screenplay	Contains mainly dialogue and directions for the action; special rules for margins and font size give a standard length of approximately one page to one minute of screen-time

☞ **Genre describes *content*, or *subject matter*.**

Genres contain certain characteristic elements. A western usually includes a gunfight. Science fiction often includes imaginary scientific developments like interstellar spaceships. A romance is always complicated with misunderstandings and difficulties.

Forms and genres are combined in various ways. For example, an epistolary novel, a novel told through letters, is a combination of two forms. Such a novel could be written in any genre and genres can be combined. A science fiction story might also be a romance, and an historical novel might also be a detective story. Also, elements of one genre are sometimes used in a different genre.

There are many possible combinations of form and genre. The following chart shows a few of the more common examples.

Some Common Examples of Form and Genre Combinations

	Examples of Forms		Examples of Genres
Fiction	Poetry	Metrical Free verse Sonnet	Epic Ballad Lyric
	Prose	Play Musical Motion picture Shakespearean Modern	Tragedy Comedy
		Novel Novella Short story	Historical Detective Fantasy Science fiction Realistic
Non-fiction		History	Political Social Military
		Biography Autobiography Memoir	
		Documentary film	
		Essay	Expository Persuasive Research
		Letter	Personal Business Letter to the editor
		Diary	
		References	Encyclopedia Dictionary Thesaurus Atlas
		Textbook Manual	

☞ **The choice of form depends on the author's purpose and on the intended audience.**

The Short Story

If an author writes, "The king died and then the queen died," the author has only provided information about an event. But if an author writes, "The king died and then the queen died of grief," the author has provided a plot line for a story. A plot is a causal sequence of events, the "why" for the things that happen in the story. The plot draws the reader into the characters' lives and helps the reader understand the decisions they make.

A plot's structure organizes the story elements. Writers vary structure depending on the needs of the story. For example, in a mystery, the author will often hold back information about the plot until later in the story. In William Faulkner's "A Rose for Emily" we only learn what Miss Emily has been doing in her mansion at the end of the story. Often narratives, such as mysteries, will begin with a "hook" that lures the reader into the story, making him or her want to know what happens next. We can talk of the location of these narrative elements as features of the plot structure.

What Goes into a Plot?

Plot structures need to have content as well. The reader wants to know both *where* in the narrative a particular event takes place, and *what* in fact happened. Authors use different ways to describe the events through which their characters pass. This variety in the telling of the story also helps to hold the reader's interest throughout the narrative.

1. **Exposition:** the information needed to understand a story. An exposition often takes place when the action of the story pauses for a moment while the narrator provides background information that is necessary for us to understand the action that is about to proceed.

2. **Complication:** the major conflict around which the story turns. A narrative may begin simply enough, with someone (Jake) going about their everyday errands. If another person (Johnny) crashes into this person's vehicle and then runs, we can say that this crash provides a complication in the otherwise regular action of conducting errands.

3. **Climax:** the turning point in the story that occurs when characters try to resolve the complication. If Jake pursues Johnny, but Johnny turns out to be armed, the climax of the story could involve a stand-off when police officers arrive on the scene.

4. **Resolution:** the set of events that bring the story to a close. To follow our example, one resolution could include Johnny agreeing to drop his gun and pay for Jake's expenses involved with the car crash.

Narrators often do not tell their stories in a straight line from the beginning to the end as these four points imply. In Ernest Hemingway's "The Short Happy Life of Francis Macomber," the action shifts from past to present. This shifting of time, called "flashback," is the way we learn what happened and why. This information gives the narrative a sense of psychological realism, helping us to understand the characters' motivations, and the emotions they express. Stretching out the information in this way keeps us curious about what is happening and draws us farther into the story.

Point of View

In our simple story, one car crashes into another. Both drivers jump out of their cars. One flees, the other pursues. A few minutes later a policeman appears, and questions several of the bystanders who saw what happened. Each person describes the accident differently based on what he or she remembers most clearly. In short stories, an author intentionally decides who tells the story and how it will be told. The tone and feel of the story, and even its meaning, can change radically depending on who is telling the story. Sometimes the narrator is intentionally made to be unreliable, leaving the readers to piece together the events of the story as best as we can. Creating an unreliable narrator does not mean the author has been negligent in writing the story and not caring about what information is included in the narrative. On the contrary, the author has to carefully control what information gets released in the story structure. The fact that a story is always told by someone, means that it is always "mediated" in some way. In a narrative we never receive the pure event, but a re-telling of that event. Think about one of the short stories you have read. Who is telling the story? Can you tell from what point of view the story is told? Does this point of view change in the story, or is it static?

Objective Point of View

With the objective point of view, the writer tells what happens without stating more than can be inferred from the story's action and dialogue. The narrator never discloses anything about what the characters think or feel, and remains a detached observer.

Third Person Point of View

Here the narrator does not participate in the action of the story as one of the characters, but lets us know exactly how the characters feel. We learn about the characters through this outside voice.

First Person Point of View

In the first person point of view, the narrator participates in the action of the story. When reading stories in the first person, we need to realize that what the narrator is recounting might not be the objective truth. We should question the trustworthiness of the accounting.

Omniscient and Limited Omniscient Points of View

A narrator who knows everything about all the characters is "all- knowing," or "omniscient." A narrator whose knowledge is limited to one character, either major or minor, has a limited omniscient point of view.

Consider some of these questions as you read one of the short stories in your text book. How does the point of view affect your responses to the characters? Do you feel sympathetic to the narrator? Do you resist what he or she is saying, or do you not feel strongly either way? How is your response influenced by how much the narrator knows and how objective he or she tries to be? First person narrators are not always trustworthy. It is up to you to determine what is the truth and what is not.

Characters

Although characters are only constructions made of language and the writer's imagination, memorable characters come alive for us while we read. While we are in the world of the text, we may experience them, and feel for them as clearly as we do our friends and family, even after we have put the book down. This is the power of a well-written story. How can we better understand the characters we meet in stories?

Learning About Characters

Characters can be distinguished as either major or minor and either static (unchanging) or dynamic (changing), though often stories will have some combination of these. Authors are not concerned with these categories when they write their stories. However, as readers we find them useful because they give us terms so that we can talk about these stories intelligently.

Contrary to what we might expect, the most important character in a story does not have to be very well known, or even present very often. In William Faulkner's "A Rose for Emily," Emily Grierson spends most of her time inside her home. The story is generated partially from her staying outside of public view, since it is told from the point of view of the townspeople who speculate about her welfare without coming into contact with her. Emily does not change as the story progresses, yet she remains the central figure in the narrative.

Perhaps the most significant aspect of a character, apart from whether they are dynamic or static, public or private, is his or her emotions. More than the action that takes place in the story, the feelings of the characters help us understand and empathize with them, as we might with friends. As Nathaniel Hawthorne says, "Blessed are all the emotions be they dark or bright." The emotions of the characters are what drive them forward. Emotions not only result from actions that take place in a story, but often cause these actions as well.

Setting

Another significant feature of the narrative includes the environment within which the events of the narrative take place. Eudora Welty states,

> "Every story would be another story, and unrecognizable if it took up its characters and plot and happened somewhere else. . . . Fiction depends for its life on place. Place is the crossroads of circumstance, the proving ground of 'What happened? Who's here? Who's coming?'"

Although we may conventionally see the setting as the background against which the important events take place, in fact the story's setting plays an active role in shaping the plot, and guiding the story to its conclusion. The setting of the story contributes a set of assumptions and a system of values that a reader may recognize without having to read through pages of explanation.

For example, if a story is set in a rural area, among the livestock and machinery of farms, we might well expect a different set of values to be in play than if the story were set in the core of a large city, among the crowds and traffic of an urban setting.

We can see the contribution a setting makes to a story by reading William Faulkner's "A Rose for Emily." This story describes the experiences of a member of an aristocratic class in the southern United States, during a time when the aristocratic class was losing much of its economic power. The narrator, who knows Miss Emily Grierson almost as "well" as we do, gives us valuable information about Miss Emily by simply describing the house in which she lives. This description helps us picture the decline of Miss Emily's influence in this town. By inference, we also learn about Miss Emily's resistance to change along with the changing economic climate:

> "It was a big, squarish frame house that had once been white, decorated with cupolas and spires and scrolled balconies in the heavily lightsome style of the seventies, set on what had once been our most select street. But garages and cotton gins had encroached and obliterated even the august names of that neighborhood; only Miss Emily's house was left, lifting its stubborn and coquettish decay above the cotton wagons and the gasoline pumps—an eyesore among eyesores."

The setting becomes linked with the values, ideals, and attitudes of that place at that time. The fact that this house has become an anachronism, helps Faulkner emphasize the Grierson's fading influence, without having to spend any valuable space actually explaining this for the reader.

Media Communications

Our world of visual media requires us to expand our definitions of "texts" and what it means to read them. Visual media conveys information in the form of images that print once conveyed. Although we may have learnt how to read books at an early age, to a certain extent the many non-verbal ways of transmitting information encourage us to learn how to read all over again. How can we better understand the visual, or graphic, text?

First, we can ask why we are being asked to look at this particular image. In addressing this question we should focus on the relation of the graphic image to the verbal content on the page. Are the two supposed to be related in some way? In what ways does the graphic convey or contrast with the verbal information?

Second, we can ask about the condition of the image at which we are looking. Has the image been modified by a graphic artist to convey a certain message? Does it depict a 'natural' scene, of people or the outdoors? Has the graphic been created as an original design by the artist? What choices in colours, sizes and shapes did the artist make? Why do you think these were used?

Third, we can think of the image as an essay. What kind of essay would you write about this image? What argument or idea do you think the image represents? Is this image really worth 'a thousand words'? In many ways, our constant saturation with images everyday makes us more skilled viewers than we may realize. What different levels of meaning do you recognize in this image? Do you like this image? Can you find any tension or examples of conflict within the image? If so, what are they? What is their source? How are they represented? What nouns, verbs and adjectives could be used to describe the image? Does the creator use any 'literary' devices, such as repetition, symbols, or puns? If so, what are they, and how do they work in the image?

Motion Pictures

Introduction

A movie consists of a series of photographs on film, projected in rapid succession onto a screen with a light and a lens. Since images remain in the eye for a fraction of a second after they are gone, the series of still photographs appear to show the smooth motion of people or objects. This phenomenon is called "persistence of vision," and explains why films are also called "motion pictures."

Making a motion picture requires contributions from a range of artists and technicians. Musicians, designers, builders, costume-makers, photographers, among many others, all collaborate in the making of a movie as well. Despite the high cost and large number of people that are necessary to make a film, probably no other art form has become as popular or influential in the twentieth-century.

The motion picture has recently become accepted as "fine art." During its early years, few people thought movies would become an art form because it required so much involvement from business interests to fund this expensive venture. Movies were also criticized because so many 'average' people loved them. They were not "high brow" enough for some critics to call "art." Movies were criticized for their reliance on technology. Surely a product that did not rely on simple tools like paint brushes and a canvass, but instead needed film and cameras and projectors and theatres, could hardly be considered art. Finally, movies were criticized because so many people were involved in movie production. It was almost impossible to single out one person who was responsible for a movie, in the same way one could identify an author for a book, or a composer for a piece of music. After the middle of the twentieth-century, however, more people began to consider movies as a legitimate form of artistic expression, similar to other fine arts such as the theatre, literature, dance, music and the visual arts.

More recently, education systems have recognized that movies are influential mediums where narratives are told. Since movies tell stories like other forms of literature, they can be considered important enough for us to "read" their themes and content, just as we would read any other literary work.

Film Genres

Like narratives, most movies can be organized into genres according to the type of story that they tell. Recognizing the genre of a movie can help us understand it better, and help us recognize symbols that may be rich in meaning for that particular type of story.

For example, if we are watching a Western, we recognize that traditionally at high noon, the villain and the hero square off. We know that this time of day is rich in meaning for the Western, because this is when justice issues are addressed in this genre of story. If we were watching a Romance, however, we know that high noon does not hold much meaning in this kind of story. Instead, midnight marks the time when the most intriguing events tend to happen—events that may have implications for what happens later in the light of day.

How can we recognize a particular kind of genre? The following are some of the features we can look for.

1. Characterization

What types of characters, stereotypes, roles, personal qualities and motivations are common in this movie? Is the film set among the rich or the poor? Does the film have characters who are supposed to represent 'average' people?

2. Filming Techniques

What stylistic conventions prevail in the film? These techniques can include:

- Camerawork – are most of the camera shots close-ups, or are they panoramas shot from a distance?
- Lighting – what palette of colours does the film use, is the atmosphere bright or dingy?
- Sound-recording – are there lots of bands contributing songs, does a single composer create the orchestral score?

Although audiences tend to be more aware of the film's story, a more sophisticated response to a movie includes many other additional features that contribute to its overall effect, either good or bad.

3. Iconography

This term refers to a familiar stock of images or motifs in the film. These motifs are primarily visual and include features like the design of the buildings, the costumes and objects, familiar patterns of dialogue, characteristic music and sounds. These motifs help to situate the movie in a particular time period, or underscore other messages that the story is attempting to convey.

4. Narrative

This term identifies similar, expected story plots, like many of the films that are produced out of Hollywood. These predictable story-lines include situations, sequences, episodes, obstacles, conflicts and resolutions.

5. Themes

We can ask about the subject matter that the movie appears to be about. What social, cultural, psychological, professional, political, sexual, moral values are addressed in the movie?

Watching a Film

We often enjoy getting 'lost' in a film that we enjoy, allowing the story to carry us along to its conclusion. However, if we are going to write successful responses to films that we watch as school assignments, we need to develop the ability to do two things at once: continue to enjoy good movies; become aware of why we enjoy them.

Initial response

To what genre would you initially assign this movie? Did you change your mind as the movie's story unfolded? If so, does the movie bring together several features from many genres? Do you think the movie intentionally brought in different features from other genres to draw you in to the story?

Previous experience

We can become aware of previous movies that we have seen in a similar genre. Can you remember the title and characters from these other, similar, movies? Did you enjoy them? A previous experience with a kind of movie may pre-dispose you to be uncritical of this film, or too critical.

Content

We can also ask about the messages that are being conveyed by the characters in the movie. What subject matter and themes are represented in the movie? What knowledge of this subject matter do you bring to this film?

The 'Grammar' of Film

Plot

We call the action that we see on screen the "plot." We do not usually see day-to-day activity in fictional narrative. The "plot" includes all those aspects of the film that advance the narrative, whether they are or are not experienced by the characters in the film. The director includes only those events that are relevant to the action of the film. These events are linked together by a chain of cause and effect. Some can be linked purely by chance, some by the intentions of the characters. Either way, the range and depth of information that we as audience members see in the movie we can call the plot. The plot is simply the material that advances the narrative.

One of the features of the plot in a movie is the depiction of background information. This background could include landscape (and other) shots, parts of the soundtrack (those not audible by the characters), and text that is printed on screen.

Story

Everything that we see or do not see that is part of the lives of the characters is called the "story." When we watch a conventional film, we see the plot, as we previously discussed. We may also perform other, more psychoanalytical functions while watching the movie. We imagine things taking place that are not (or not yet) part of the plot. We imagine that a particular person is the diamond thief. We presume that due to the characters' clean clothes and the shining sun a new day has begun. All of this information that we infer about the characters' lives we call the "story."

Film uses certain common conventions often referred to as the 'grammar' of these audiovisual media. These conventions perform a similar organizational function for film as does conventional grammar structures for language. This list includes some of the most important conventions for conveying meaning through particular camera and editing techniques (as well as some of the specialized vocabulary of film production). Conventions are not rules: expert practitioners manipulate them for deliberate effect, which is one of the rare occasions when we become aware of what the convention is.

Editing Techniques

Cut is a sudden change of shot from one viewpoint or location to another. On television, cuts occur on average about every 7 or 8 seconds. Cutting may either change the scene, compress time, vary the point of view, or build up an image or idea. The director always has a reason for a cut. Asking yourself the reason for a particular kind of edit can help you better understand other aspects of the narrative as well. Less abrupt transitions are achieved with techniques known as fades, dissolves, and wipes.

Doing Time

1. Screen time

Screen time refers to a period of time that is represented by events within a film. Do the events in a film take place over the course of a week or several years?

2. Subjective time

This term refers to the time experienced or felt by a character in a film. This way of depicting time shows, for example, time stretching as a person flees from a dangerous situation. Ironically, time is stretched in the film because of the character's desire for it to be compressed.

3. Compressed time

This term refers to the compression of time between sequences or scenes, and within scenes. Compressing time is the most commonly used means of manipulating time, and it is practiced with cuts or dissolves. In a dramatic narrative, for example, if a person's climb up a staircase does not contribute to the plot, a shot of a character starting up the stairs may then cut to him entering a room. The logic of the situation and our past experience of watching films tells us that the room is somewhere at the top of the stairs. Long journeys of several days can be compressed into seconds with this same technique.

4. Flashback

As with written narratives, flashbacks in film break the chronology of a narrative in which events from the past are shown to the viewer. The convention often used to indicate a flashback has been a gradual blur or a ripple dissolve.

Internet

Introduction

Of the many new texts we must learn how to read, perhaps none demands more immediate attention than the Internet, as it has become a popular source of information. The reading skills we need for the text of internet web sites are similar to those we use when reading traditional literature. These skills are especially necessary for us to determine the quality and reliability of the information found on the internet.

How To Read a Web Site

Viewing web sites may seem to be a very different activity from reading literature. However, in many important ways both reading practices are very similar. You should ask yourself some questions that will help you to determine the validity and reliability of the information presented on a web site. Consider the following:

1. We should ask questions about the author of the site, since the author's professional background lends credibility to the content that is posted on the site. Does the site post information about the author of the materials that are found there? Does the author have training or recognized expertise in the field that the web site represents?

2. We should ask questions about the content on the site. Is the information consistent with information from other sources such as books or other web sites? Usually academic publishers are reliable sources of information about a subject. Is the information easy to understand? Does the site present more than one side of an issue?

3. We should ask about the intended audience for this site. Does the author seem to have a specific audience in mind? Does the site have advertisements? If so, what do the advertisements suggest about the intended audience? How has the site been funded— through corporate sponsorships, or through non-profit organizations? Will these companies also want to reach you?

4. We should ask questions about the structure of the site. Is it easy to navigate? Can you exit at any time? Can you go back to a previous page without hitting the 'back' button on the browser? Are there links to other sites that give you additional information?

5. We should ask about the site's relevance to the work that you are doing. Sometimes you may find a well-constructed and informative site as you conduct research on the web. However, the information that the site presents does not really relate to the work that you are doing. Instead of becoming confused by trying to relate this information to your work, it may often be wiser, and less time-consuming, to search for a more relevant website.

The Novel

Narratives are stories. It is important to know how to read stories because they serve many important purposes in our world. Advertisers and politicians use stories to persuade us. Novelists often use stories to examine various ideas. We use narratives to re-tell the events of a day to a friend. We can also use narratives to discover how non-narrative texts, such as magazine essays and editorials, convey meaning. By comparing narrative and non-narrative texts, we notice how narratives tend to be organized by their characters and non-narrative works tend to be organized by their arguments. Non-narrative texts tend to be based on abstractions like ideas and reasons. Narrative texts may be based on abstract ideas as well, such as family relationships, but explore these ideas through the lives of people represented in the story.

Reading Narratives

A novel is one type of narrative. Since novels can be complex and sophisticated, we can approach them from several different angles. One angle focuses on the purposes of the characters that shape the narrative. Gaining a sense of the purpose that shapes the text has a direct bearing on the way you would read. To discover the purpose in the narrative we ask ourselves questions about the characters and their actions. As the narrative progresses, the characters begin to address our questions. Often the characters and their actions give suggestions and clues to our questions that we can pursue further in our reading.

A second approach to reading focuses on the design of the narrative. Although this approach ignores the characters' 'lives', we can still recognize its significance by trying to imagine a story without any formal elements. Even the stories we tell each other about the events of our day are organized in some way, by grammar, action, rhythm, by the selection of information. Written narratives are no different than our spoken stories in this way. Plot, characterization, tone, point of view, dialogue, duration, imagery and descriptions all demonstrate the author's hand in designing and shaping his narrative. None of these narrative elements are self-evident in a story. Each of them is carefully selected by the author to heighten the story's effectiveness. In this approach to reading we do not accept that a story could be 'natural', or exist apart from the intention of its author.

A third way of reading focuses on the events the characters of the narrative pass through. This technique is similar to the first one discussed. Here, we look more specifically for what the characters learn from their experiences. Readers who favour this approach may defend it by arguing that both characters and readers share language as the means for describing their circumstances. They may also argue that characterization, instead of design, makes stories interesting because characters let us see something of ourselves in what they do. This approach to reading lets us consider the ethical or philosophical implications of the characters' actions in the narrative. Since the characters are only fictitious, no harm or benefit takes place in the physical world as a result of their actions. Readers can 'watch' from a distance and evaluate based on their own understanding of similar experiences.

Other approaches can also be used to deepen our understanding of narratives. For example, we could draw out the sequence of events of a narrative text using a flow chart. By drawing a diagram, we can organize the progression of events in order, even though the narrative itself may tell them in a non-chronological order. Identifying the sequence of events can also help us understand the motivations of characters who act or speak in certain ways.

Describing the sequence of events can also lead to a clearer understanding of the relationships between characters and the events that led to their formation or dissolution.

Keeping the following questions in mind may give you further insights into the narrative you are reading. These questions may bring others to mind. You may find it useful to keep a pen and paper handy while reading to jot down your questions. On the other hand, you may prefer to enjoy an uninterrupted time with your book, writing out questions and responses when you are finished.

1. Did this event affect the characters and/or the direction of the story in significant ways?

2. Did the character make any important decisions at this point in the story? What were they? Why did the character make these decisions?

3. What other decisions could they have made?

4. What would the outcome for the narrative have been if the character had made different decisions at this point?

5. What effect does the character's decision have on the other members of the story? Is the character aware of the effect this decision will have on the others? Does the character hesitate before taking this particular action?

6. Does the character's decision help us to understand something about the character's personality?

7. What scenario does the narrator open the story that you are reading? Are there any images that may have significance in the story that follows? Do the final events of the narrative entice you to reread any parts of the story?

Drama

Drama is similar to prose fiction in many ways. Both genres can be classified as narratives, and both utilize similar narrative techniques. Novels and plays are both narrative genres. Although plays perform their narratives instead of telling them, they tend to be organized by plots, just like other narrative genres. Plays also feature the passing of time on two levels. The one level of duration represents the passing of time of the performance. The other level represents the passing of time in the play itself.

But how similar is a play to a novel or a poem? We can distinguish the dramatic text from other literary forms because of its orientation toward public performance. None of the other literary forms in the fiction and the poetry sections are created with a live audience in mind. The text of a play may be viewed as a guide to a performance, comparable to a blueprint, a musical score, or even a recipe for a cake. The role of the audience is an integral part of the text because the audience provides an immediate response to the performers.

We can distinguish the two genres from each other through their usual mode of reception: plays are performed publicly and novels tend to be read privately. Although this difference between them is the most obvious, there are several other differences. For example, a novelist can more easily supply information on historical backgrounds, be spatially mobile, and present summaries. The novelist can also filter the story through the point of view of one or more characters, and express a character's inner life more easily than the playwright. In drama, soliloquies and asides can fulfill some of these functions, but they are less convenient to integrate into the performance, and can become intrusive if used too often.

There are other non-textual elements that distinguish the drama from other genres. Although a dramatic performance features the actors on stage, many other people work behind the scenes to ensure that the dramatic narrative is 'told' as effectively as possible. Because of the range of involvement from other fields, including carpentry, light, graphic and sound designers, a drama can be considered a multi-media text. Scripts not only include the dialogue of the characters, but they also include directions for the set designers, the lighting designers and the sound designers. Audiences use both their visual and auditory senses. To coordinate all the elements of a performed drama, several other people are involved beyond the original author, or playwright. The following are some examples.

- A **director** stages the play, developing the concept of the production, and conducting the rehearsals. The director is usually responsible for and credited with a production, typically designated as his or her production.

- A **producer** or theater manager is responsible for managing the financial aspects of a production, hiring actors, and selling tickets. A good producer has to recognize a potentially great piece of theatre as well as find the money to stage it.

- A **stage manager** is in charge of the performance itself, and co-ordinates all backstage activity.

Reading the Dramatic Text

Some people suggest that a play is not really a play until it is actually performed on a stage before an audience. In this view, the dramatic text is meant to be performed and simply reading the play does not allow one to understand the subtle complexities of the dramatic text. For our purpose we recognize both the importance of live performance in shaping a dramatic narrative and we also recognize the importance of private readings in understanding a dramatic narrative. This approach assumes that we could be both readers who read with a view to performance, and theatergoers who watch plays that we have read. We should accept the text, therefore, as both a piece of literature and as a guide to performance. Like a director, we should be able to bring the play to life in our imaginations.

How would we read a dramatic narrative then? One useful way to read a play is for its potential to be performed on a stage. Even though you may have never considered how to stage a play before, you can think about how you would design the set and costumes of a particular play, based on the events that take place in the narrative between the characters on stage. This approach helps you to recognize the traditional features of narrative (such as foreshadowing, symbolism, conflict resolution), as well as the specific features of the performed text (such as period costumes, lighting effects, setting). The decisions that you would make as you try to stage a play would all be influenced by what is happening in the play itself.

Practice Assignment - Light and Dark Imagery in Romeo and Juliet

If your essay assignment was to discuss the significance of light and dark imagery in William Shakespeare's Romeo and Juliet, you could begin by noting the prevalence of this imagery throughout the play. In this case you would not be reading the play as a performed text, but as a literary one, much like you would read any narrative. For example, in the first scene, Lady Montague tells Benvolio that she is glad Romeo did not take part in the brawl, and asks if he's seen him. Benvolio answers, "Madam, an hour before the worshipp'd sun / Peer'd forth the golden window of the east, / A troubled mind drave me to walk abroad . . . ." (1.1.118-120). Benvolio then says that Romeo has been avoiding the light because of his melancholy mood:

> *Many a morning hath he there been seen,*
> *With tears augmenting the fresh morning dew,*
> *Adding to clouds more clouds with his deep sighs;*
> *But all so soon as the all-cheering sun*
> *Should in the furthest east begin to draw*
> *The shady curtains from Aurora's bed,*
> *Away from the light steals home my heavy son. . .*
> *Black and portentous must this humor prove,*
> *Unless good counsel may the cause remove. (1.1.131-142)*

Benvolio, whose own restlessness causes him to rise before the sun, notes how "black and portentous" Romeo's preference for darkness could become, if "good counsel" cannot remedy Romeo's brooding.

Although this example appears early in the play, we notice many more references to light and dark as we read further. Capulet invites Paris to the feast with the words: "At my poor house look to behold this night / Earth-treading stars that make dark heaven light" (1.2.24-25). The "Earth-treading stars" metaphorically describe the beautiful women who will attend, shining so brightly that they will figuratively light up the night sky. Glowing light symbolizes feminine beauty at the end of the scene as well. Romeo resists Benvolio's attempts at getting him to forget his first girlfriend, Rosaline, with an image of light: "The all-seeing sun / Ne'er saw her match since first the world begun" (1.2.92-93). Benvolio replies that at Capulet's feast he will see "shining" (1.2.98). Not persuaded, Romeo declares that he will go to the feast, "no such sight to be shown, / But to rejoice in splendor of mine own" (1.2.101). "Splendor" describes dazzling beauty, but its root meaning derives from a word meaning "intense light."

Furthermore, when Romeo meets, not Rosaline, but Juliet, his exclamation relies heavily on the familiar light imagery: "O, she doth teach the torches to burn bright! It seems she hangs upon the cheek of night" (1.5.44-46). Romeo describes Juliet through an image of light, stating that her beauty is brighter than the blaze of any torch. In fact, light images seem to collect whenever Juliet's name is mentioned. Do you remember Romeo's well-known speech upon seeing Juliet come to the window? "But, soft! what light through yonder window breaks? / It is the east, and Juliet is the sun" (2.2.2-3). He continues with the same extended metaphor of light and dark: "Arise, fair sun, and kill the envious moon, / Who is already sick and pale with grief, / That thou her maid art far more fair than she" (2.2.4-6).

As you might expect, when Friar Laurence appears, he helps us understand the complexity of Romeo and Juliet's situation through a metaphor of light: "The grey-eyed morn smiles on the frowning night, / Chequering the eastern clouds with streaks of light, / And fleckled [dappled] darkness like a drunkard reels / From forth day's path and Titan's fiery wheels" (2.3.1-4). In contrast with Romeo's description of Juliet as filled with pure light, Friar Laurence's description of light is tinged with darkness: the morning is "grey-eyed." The eastern clouds are "chequered," and "streaked," and the fading night is described as "fleckled." Equating the rising sun to the "fiery wheels" of the god, Titan, foreshadows the tragic, or dark, ending that we can expect from these "star-cross'd" lovers.

This more complex version of the light metaphor recurs when Friar Laurence returns to the play at the end. He inquires about the light that shines in Romeo's tomb: "Tell me, good my friend, /What torch is yond, that vainly lends his light /To grubs and eyeless skulls? as I discern, /It burneth in the Capel's monument." The putrefaction and death found in the tomb is linked with the night-time darkness that no human-made light could overcome. We might initially think of the weakness of a human torch in the face of night-time darkness as representing human mortality, always succumbing to death. However, in this context we could make a stronger connection between the flickering light and the dubious scheme the friar had proposed for Romeo and Juliet to escape the hatred of each others' families.

And just in case you had missed the significance of the metaphor for light in these earlier passages of the play, it turns up one last time in the Prince's speech, following the discovery of the dead bodies in Romeo's tomb: "A glooming peace this morning with it brings;/ The sun, for sorrow, will not show his head." The prince's words also contrast with Romeo's earlier description of Juliet as the sun, making the sky brighten in the east. Now, at the play's conclusion, the conflict that kept the Montagues' and Capulets' at daggers with each other finally has been resolved, but the peace is a "glooming peace." The cost of this resolution has been the lives of two young people who were full of hope and promise.

You will remember that we have run through "Romeo and Juliet" because of a hypothetical assignment. This assignment asked us to discuss the significance of light and dark imagery in this play, and our approach was to notice how often this imagery turns up. We could have selected many other passages from the text that draw on a light metaphor. A strong essay goes beyond identifying the number of times the metaphor appears in the play. It explains how the metaphor contributes to, or enriches, the meaning of the narrative.

The Essay

Ever since the rise of magazine publishing in the nineteenth-century, the essay genre has become increasingly popular. The term "essay" comes from the French "essais," which simply means "attempt." Many of these early published "attempts," were what we would call informal essays, a collection of thoughts on an everyday subject. Magazines today, such as *The New Yorker* and *The Atlantic Monthly*, are comprised of informal essays. In school, the genre studied most often is the formal essay. In the formal essay, the author attempts to advance an argument. The arguments can be relatively significant, such as the reasons for global warming. Or, they can be relatively insignificant, such as the status of a rock band. Formal essays of these kinds can be read in magazines such *as Scientific American* and *Rolling Stone*. The formal essay that you write is similar to the formal essays that are published in magazines: a formal essay doesn't use colloquial language, nor contractions like the one in this sentence. It is characterized by language that is suitable for conducting an academic argument, and maintaining a sober and thoughtful tone.

The essay genre has two main categories: informal and formal. To more clearly understand the essay's function, the genre can be categorized according to what it attempts to do.

Narrative Essay

- Describes what happened and when.
- Emphasizes the chronological order of events.
- Uses transitional words to make the description flow more smoothly.
- The point of view shapes the voice, tone, and purpose of the story.
- The mood guides the reader's response.
- The tone of the writing helps the reader to understand what the event meant to the author.

Definition Essay

- Describes an object or defines an abstract term.
- The author of a definition essay can use a variety of techniques to express the meaning of an object or term. Negation can be used to clarify what the word does not mean. Focusing on the origins of the word shows how its meaning has changed throughout different historical contexts. Illustrations can demonstrate what the word has meant to different people. Although a dictionary provides definitions of terms, these are sometimes short and cryptic, leaving us wanting to know more about the term. Often an encyclopedia provides definition essays that help us understand the broader context within which a difficult term is used.

Classification Essay

- Describes the object or terms into categories that show its relation to other objects or terms.
- Sometimes a scientist writes an essay that classifies certain phenomena based on the research that has been conducted in the laboratory. This kind of essay is usually best appreciated by others in the same field who understand the categories that the author uses to classify the information.

Process Analysis Essay

- Describes how it happened.

- The process analysis essay describes the sequence of events that took place to produce a certain result. Like the Classification Essays, often these are best appreciated by others who are also in the same field. Therefore, when writing Process Analysis essays, you need to be aware of the audience who will be reading your work, and use terms that will be understood by this audience. The best rule of thumb to use at all times is to use the simplest language possible to convey your information.

Cause and Effect Essay

- Describes why it happened.

- Like the Process Analysis essay, the Cause and Effect essay describes the sequence of events that led to the consequence in question. This essay format, however, focuses more closely on the individual steps that led to the final result.

Persuasion Essay

- Describes why a person would want to do something.

- The opening paragraph of a persuasion essay often determines whether the reader will continue reading your work or move on to the next essay. Essays such as Process Analysis, and Cause and Effect appeal to the reader's rational faculties, but the Persuasion essay appeals to a reader's emotional faculties. The logic that you use must be sound in order to make your argument effective. However, the examples that you use should be drawn from an emotional source, to convince your reader of the plausibility of your position.

Compare and Contrast Essay

- Describes the similarities and differences between various phenomena.

- Comparison and contrast essays are often difficult for us to write because they require that we organize our work more carefully than the other essay forms. In order for the reader to follow along with you, it's important to make sure that you provide markers in your text to signal when you are comparing the similarities of various items and when you are contrasting them. The reader should also have no difficulty understanding which of your items you are talking about. As before, the clearer your language, the stronger your argument.

Example Essay

- Describes an example of events that have taken place which are considered worthy of note. Most example essays use specific examples that express the abstract idea that you are arguing. These examples should be described briefly, but in detail, so that the reader can easily understand the application being made between this occasion and the abstraction that is represented.

Sample Student Essay: Oliver Twist, by Charles Dickens

The word "essay" comes from the French "essais" which simply means "an attempt." Let's take a moment to consider one student's "attempt," written on Charles Dickens' *Oliver Twist*. After reading the essay, think about the aspects of this piece that you liked, and the aspects you think could be improved. Compare your thoughts to the strengths and weaknesses of this writing that are found at the conclusion of the essay.

Art and Politics in Charles Dickens' *Oliver Twist*

1   Charles Dickens published Oliver Twist in 1883 to express the need for social reform, identifying the abuses of laborers in workhouses. Dickens does not attempt to romanticize this situation in order to appeal to more readers and increase the sales of his book. Instead he describes the harsh realities of a bad place at a bad time: an English workhouse just after the Poor Law Act of 1834.

2   The description of the experience of laboring in an English workhouse at this time shifts abruptly from one mood to another, from comedy to pathos. Like on a dramatic stage, the scene shifts from that of a drunken woman to the dying mother and finally to the hardened doctor. Such rapid shifts work on several levels, contributing both variety and unity and creating both comedy and pathos, a multi-pronged effect Dickens admired in melodrama. In this first chapter, Dickens also captures life and death in a single sentence, "Let me see the child, and die." (Dickens, 2). This sums up the mother's will to see the newborn baby, and takes a short stride from birth to death.

3   Dickens attempts to create his characters in a way that seems realistic to the reader. His characters appear to be people with whom the reader can sympathize. Thus when the character falls under the influence of a harmful environment the reader may feel the tension of knowing that an action is bad, while at the same time understanding its motivation. For example, many of the characters in Oliver Twist attempt to free themselves from a dispiriting economic situation. Sometimes they are obliged to do so through illegal means. However, the startling exception to these attempts rests in the experience of Oliver himself. Since Oliver is portrayed in the narrative as innocent, he becomes inured to the harmful effects of the environment around him. As in many novels where the hero receives an education, Oliver's ability to withstand these harmful effects develops as he faces tests on his sense of goodness.

4   Oliver is carefully manipulated by a band of thieves. First they cunningly cold-shoulder and isolate him, then they cunningly bring him back into the deadly warmth of their family circle. Since Oliver wanted to belong to a family of some kind, even if it wasn't biological, he was glad to make himself useful to the gang. He was also happy to have recognizable faces to see daily, even if they were those of petty criminals. So he expresses his readiness to help out members of the gang. He kneels on the floor before Dodger and takes his foot in his lap. He begins a process that Mr. Dawkins called "japanning his trotter-cases," which also means, "cleaning his boots."

5   As we know, Oliver finally escapes this situation but he is still threatened by another danger. Early Victorian society, the society of free economy without many social programs, tended to take individual privacy for granted. Most families felt almost hostile toward interference from outside influences. This lack of a sense of public responsibility may have derived from the scarcity of resources for most families at this time. However, Dickens himself does not ignore social issues in his books, but attempts to write about the difficulties in the society which he witnesses around him. He tries to unify the two worlds of politics and art.

6   Oliver Twist represents the difficulties of society during the Victorian period. Dickens does not create a dream world that panders to the needs of readers for a happy ending. Instead he bluntly describes the world as he sees it. Although Oliver Twist does not leave us with a sense of optimism and feeling of well-being, it may spark a sense of outrage in his readers' hearts towards the English workhouses. He was promoting reform by moving the people.

7   As we read Dickens' works, we can see how they were influenced by events happening around him. One main quality of Dickens' work, was that it contained many symbols to express his criticisms about society. We find the first example of this in the very first chapter of the book, as the birth of Oliver and conditions of the workhouse are described. This scene criticizes the Poor Laws of 1834 that had been instated four years earlier. In the workhouses, men, women, and children were separated, fed minimal meals, and worked like dogs.

8   Oliver Twist differs from many of Dickens' other works by its lack of the humour and wit that were featured in the two preceding novels. Instead, Oliver Twist depicts the harsh life of an orphan pitted against poverty and cruelty. More than a diversion for the public while they rode the trains, the story challenged officials to reform English laws. He wrote about what he had lived through as a child, about what he saw as he walked the streets of England in the midst of poverty and cruelty. Dickens wrote about elements that were affecting his life time: From Poor Laws to Furniture Designs to Philosophy.

On "Art and Politics in Charles Dickens' Oliver Twist"

A useful place to start thinking about this student's essay is the overall meaning that she was trying to express. We should be able to find this meaning in the opening paragraph of the essay. What information do we find in the first paragraph? The student identifies the author, title and date of the text on which she will focus her essay discussion. Doing so in the opening sentence is effective because it immediately defines the scope for the work that will follow. The phrases that follow the opening statement further narrow the scope. Since many different topics could emerge from one narrative, it's important that we state clearly at the outset of the essay the topic that is interesting to us in this novel. The student states that the author's motive for writing *Oliver Twist* was to "address the need for social reform, identifying the abuses of labourers in workhouses" (paragraph 1). From this opening phrase we can assume that the discussion to follow will focus on the representation of workers' rights in Dickens' novel. The second and third sentences confirm this assumption for us, by under-scoring the "harsh realities" of the workers in the Victorian period, and the unflinching descriptions offered in Oliver Twist.

To write a clear paper that carefully considers the representations of working class people at this time, this opening paragraph needs at least one more sentence, a thesis sentence. The thesis statement describes the actual argument that the student will present about the working conditions. Most essays need to do more than simply present information to the reader. If we could speak to this student about her paper, we would want to ask her questions like: "Why did you want to write about this particular novel?" "Is there anything about the way Dickens portrays the conditions during this time period that caught your attention?" "Do different characters in the novel appear to respond better under the difficult conditions of nineteenth-century England than others?" "Since we know that Dickens himself was doing more than simply describing the "harsh realities of a bad place at a bad time," in what ways do you think he tried to move people to change those social conditions?" "Does he imply that criminals thrive under these harsh economic conditions, while hard-working people suffer?" As you can imagine, any one of these questions could start off a long conversation with the author about the topic of her essay. We note that in this opening paragraph, this kind of specific information showing us what the author intended to do with her reading of *Oliver Twist* is missing. What we should be able to find, usually near the end of the paragraph, is a sentence that offers us both the argument, as well as the three points that will shape that argument in the text that follows.

When we move from paragraph one to paragraph two, the essay is missing a smooth transition. One of the early sentences in the first paragraph should give us the topic that organizes the discussion that follows in the next paragraph. We could take the first sentence of this second paragraph as the topic sentence, telling us that the paragraph will discuss the shift from comedy to pathos. If the author had let us know in the thesis sentence that the first point would discuss the shifts in moods throughout the novel, this first point would have deeper roots in the paper, and we as readers would be better prepared to consider the argument that follows. The shift from the end of paragraph one to the beginning of paragraph two is abrupt. The impression it gives us as readers is that it was not very thoughtfully considered by the author.

The terms "comedy" and "pathos" in the novel have rich traditions in English literature. It would be interesting to see how they could be applied to this particular novel. We could suggest the student provide more information about comedy and pathos in the novel than there currently is in the essay. A good way to begin a discussion that introduces new terms is with some provisional definitions, either from a dictionary or other reference book. Another way is to briefly introduce another prominent literary work that features one of the terms. Either way, this kind of an introduction lays the basis for a careful reading of the role that these terms play in the novel.

In this essay, however, the student gives a promising start, but the weakness in this work is that it does not go far enough. For example, we are not told why a scene involving a drunken woman would necessarily be comic. Does Dickens intend the scene to have comic elements that we would find distasteful today? We can imagine the pathos in a scene involving a dying mother, or even a hardened doctor. A successful essay needs to pause a moment to explain specifically what in these scenes evokes this sense of pathos. We could ask this student to outline the ways in which she feels this comedy and pathos relate to the idea of social reform. Is it the sudden shift in mood from the comedy to pathos that might move a reader to recognize the plight of working class people?

With these questions in mind then, it becomes apparent that when the student introduces yet another rich term, "melodrama," into the discussion, we feel that we have only briefly touched on the surface of an argument that had potential for depth and nuance. We may accept her comment that these "rapid shifts [between comedy and pathos] work on several levels." Unfortunately, the same supportive comments need to be included in this part of the essay that were in the sentences just before it. Could she describe "melodrama," as she did "comic" and "pathos"? Does Dickens give melodrama a more political purpose, than it had been used to that point in popular literature? To write a paper with a unified argument, we would repeat our earlier question about "social reform" (paragraph 1). In what ways do these features from melodrama help advance Dickens' agenda of creating better working conditions for the country's poor?

To improve the rest of this student's second paragraph, we would address her rapid shift, immediately after introducing the term "melodrama," to the "capture" of "life and death" in one notable sentence. For an argument to work in a paragraph, the information needs to relate to the information that precedes it, and that information needs to advance the argument named in the topic sentence. The term "also" does not provide a strong enough link between "melodrama" in the previous sentence, and "life and death" in the present sentence. Perhaps the student has an idea buried in her writing that could be drawn to the surface and expanded upon. It may be possible to make a link between "melodrama" and the melodramatic situation of a mother asking to see her newborn child before passing away. If the essay were to explain the ways in which this scene advances her argument, she would have effectively made her point with strong evidence from the narrative itself. We can see that the student is making intelligent choices as she writes her paper. However, we can also see how a more meticulous approach to this topic would help make the essay work more comprehensive and produce a higher mark for the student.

You may wish to try this same analysis on any one of the other paragraphs in the essay. On a blank piece of paper make a list of those aspects of her discussion that you feel are strong. On this list you could include all the levels of writing, from the grammatical structure of the sentences, to the content of the sentences, to the way these sentences are organized. Your suggestions for improvement could also include these same levels. What might you do to clarify what you think she is trying to say? From your knowledge of *Oliver Twist* what evidence would you introduce into the discussion to support the assertions that she is making? What evidence from the narrative might contradict these assertions? How would you account for this contradiction?

Narratives

All stories, or **narratives**, have certain things in common. Short stories, novels, and movies, even history books and documentaries, share certain common elements. Some elements may be more developed in one kind of narrative. Non-fiction, for example, imposes certain limits— limits like telling the truth. Most of the following elements are present in works that you read or view.

Point of View

A story always has a narrator: someone who tells the story. **Narrative point of view** describes who tells the story and how the story is told. In one sense, the real narrator is the author. However, the narrator is also one of the author's inventions, made up just as the author made up the story.

The Narrative Points of View

Point of View	How the Story is Told	Narrators
First person	The story is told by one of the characters in the story ("I"). The narrator is part of the story.	**First-person narrators** only know what they themselves think, feel, do, and see.
Third person	The story is told through the eyes of one or more characters ("he, she, they"). The narrator is outside the story, and tells what the characters think, feel, and do.	**Omniscient narrators** know about everything that happens and what any character thinks and feels. **Limited-omniscient narrators** only know about one character and the things that the one character knows, thinks, feels, and does.
Objective	The story is told without telling any characters' thoughts and feelings. Only the characters' actions and words are told. This point of view is like the camera's point of view in a film.	The **objective narrator** only knows what a camera can record. Thus this story-telling form suffers from the limitations of film—but at the same time can produce a film-like effect.

Sometimes the narrator cannot be trusted. In telling the story, the narrator may make mistakes, misunderstand things, leave things out, or tell lies. The **unreliable narrator** is a good example of the author inventing the narrator.

The narrator may sometimes address the reader directly (as in Charlotte Brontë's *Jane Eyre*, when the first-person narrator says *Reader, I married him*). While stories are commonly told without direct comment, first person narrators often comment indirectly by simply telling their thoughts.

Plot

A **plot** is made up of two things: the events of the story and the reasons for the events. Many people in telling about a book or a movie will say *X happened and then Y happened and then Z happened.* However, without knowing *why* X, Y, and Z happened, there is no plot, there is only a list of events.

☞   **The causes of events are an important part of a plot.**

Most plots also have a recognizable structure. The following plot elements can be recognized in nearly every story.

Exposition

- Introduction of characters, setting, and situation.
- Explanation of **antecedent action**, or what happened before the story started.

Complication

- Increasing **conflict.**
- **Characterization**, or development of characters.

Climax

- Culmination of the action.
- How the story will turn out.
- The turning point.

Resolution

- Final explanations and conclusion.
- Sometimes called the **denouement**, or final outcome which explains everything.
- Sometimes divided into denouement and resolution.

These plot elements are often outlined in a **plot diagram**. The unequal sides of this diagram show that the resolution is shorter than the rising action. In fact, the resolution is often *very* short.

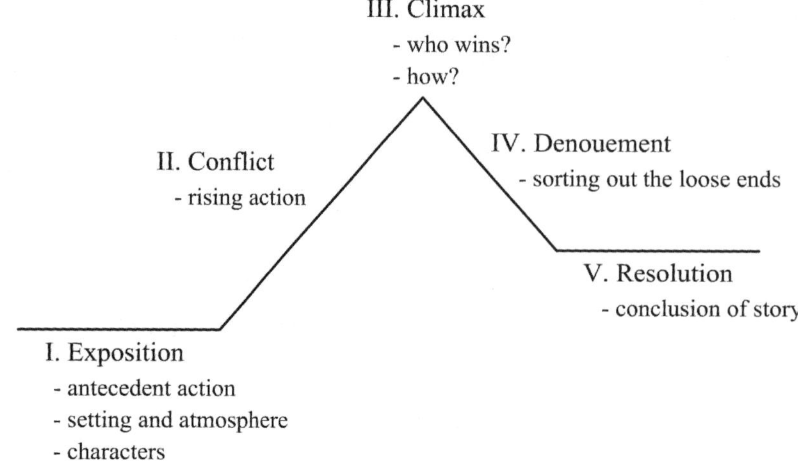

Either the plot headings or the plot diagram could be used to outline nearly everything that occurs in a short story. When studying a novel, the plot is longer and more complicated, and there may be subplots; in addition, chapters of a book can also be outlined using plot structure. As a result, a novel study might require several plot outlines: one for the plot of the overall story, one or more for subplots, and a number for plotting each chapter (or other divisions of the story).

Conflict

Stories are about people and their struggles. In a story, everything that gets in the way of characters as they struggle to get what they want produces **conflict.** Sometimes the conflict is a physical struggle or dramatic disagreements. However, conflict also exists in misunderstanding and uncertainty. In a mystery story, the mystery itself can be the conflict.

Kinds of Conflict

Internal	External
Characters struggle within **themselves**. They struggle with conscience, emotions, destructive character traits, or with conflicting desires or principles. Internal conflict can be complicated and also combined with external conflict. An inner conflict over values, for example, can be part of a conflict with society's values.	Characters may struggle with **other people** because of hatred, disagreement, or misunderstanding. There may be a struggle between good and evil. There may be conflicting ideas about what is good—a clash of ideals. It is even possible for all the characters to be working together while problems arise from "the conflict." Characters may struggle with entire groups of people—the conflict may be with **society**. Characters may struggle with **universal problems** like war, disease, poverty, or alienation. Characters may struggle with **nature** in the form of wild weather, hostile terrain, or savage animals. Characters may struggle with the **unknown,** with mysteries of any kind: ghosts, miracles, alien abductions, fate, the final mystery of death—or with the theft of a diamond necklace.

Characterization

Everything that a writer does to portray characters is called **characterization**. One of the basic methods of characterization is to invent different kinds of characters that serve different purposes.

Characters Classified by Type

Flat	Have only one quality or character trait; are one-sided; they always act the same way.
Round	Have different, even contradictory traits; are more like real people.
Stock	Are like **flat** characters, except that stock characters have been used over and over and are instantly recognizable.
Archetypal	Are like stock characters, except that **archetypes** are meant to be typical (even universal) examples of certain character traits.
Dynamic	Change or grow in some way—for good or bad, they are altered by events and by their own actions and choices.
Static	Do not change; **flat**, **round**, **stock**, and **archetypal** characters can all be static.
Foil	Used as a contrast to the main character, or protagonist; the difference between the foil and the main character emphasizes the main character's qualities; the foil is used for **indirect characterization.**

Good storytellers use all of these types of characters. The amount of characterization that a character receives is generally controlled by the character's function in the story. The most important character in a story is usually round and dynamic (or at least the writer *tries* for round and dynamic). However, the taxi driver whose only function is to delay the protagonist by taking a wrong turn is usually flat. In fact, some characters *must* be flat—there is no time or space to portray them as real people.

Characters Classified by Function

Protagonist	The main character; the protagonist is often the hero, but not always—sometimes the main character is a villain; the protagonist is often a **dynamic character.**
Antagonist	The character the protagonist struggles against; the antagonist is often the villain, but not always.
Major	Help move the plot forward in some way; they are often **round** and dynamic; the **protagonist** and **antagonist** are major characters.
Minor	Have minor roles; they affect an event in the plot, but they do not move the whole plot forward; minor characters are often **flat** or **stock** because they do not appear long enough to be fully developed.

Writers have two ways of portraying their characters. They can comment directly, or they can show their characters speaking and acting.

Methods of Characterization

Direct characterization is *told* through direct statements made by the narrator.	Indirect characterization is *shown* through actions and dialogue.
• From the narrator's statements about a character—*Jane was clever and stubborn.* • From **indirect characterization** that is obvious or contrived—as when one character says or thinks something about another character, and it sounds just like the narrator's voice—or when a character stops to look in a mirror.	• From what a character says or thinks. • From what a character says or thinks about another character. • From what a character thinks about self, others, and the world. • From what a character does. • From a character's reactions to a character.

Setting and Atmosphere

The **setting** is the *where* and *when*: present-day New York, the American South in 1850, the moon in 2135, the African veldt in the Stone Age, Renaissance Verona. When a story is carefully constructed, the setting is an important part of the work.

The setting is often chosen for a purpose. Think of the setting of the scene in Shakespeare's *Macbeth* in which Macbeth and Banquo meet the three witches: the setting is a heath, a land so infertile that it will not even support trees. A wasteland emphasizes the evil of the witches who are cut off from human society by their crimes, just as Macbeth's crimes will soon cut him off from society.

The **atmosphere** is the mood or the feeling produced by a work. The feeling of gloom, horror, and despair that afflicts Macbeth as he sinks deeper into crime is the atmosphere of the play; it is the feeling that the play produces in the audience.

The setting often contributes to the atmosphere. Sometimes both setting and atmosphere can be deliberately arranged to contrast with the events or meaning of a story.

Theme

The **theme** of any work is its subject, what the work is about. The theme can be divided into two parts: the subject itself and what is said about the subject. For example, Shakespeare's *Macbeth* is about ambition, and that ambition is pursued ruthlessly, at the cost of many lives. Shakespeare shows that once Macbeth decides to be king, he commits one crime after another to first seize the throne and then to keep it.

The theme can be described in a kind of equation.

$$\boxed{\text{subject}} \; + \; \boxed{\text{statement about the subject}} \; = \; \boxed{\text{theme}}$$

In a skillfully constructed narrative, everything contributes to the theme. Everything in the narrative is about the theme.

☛ **All the elements of the narrative contribute to the theme.**

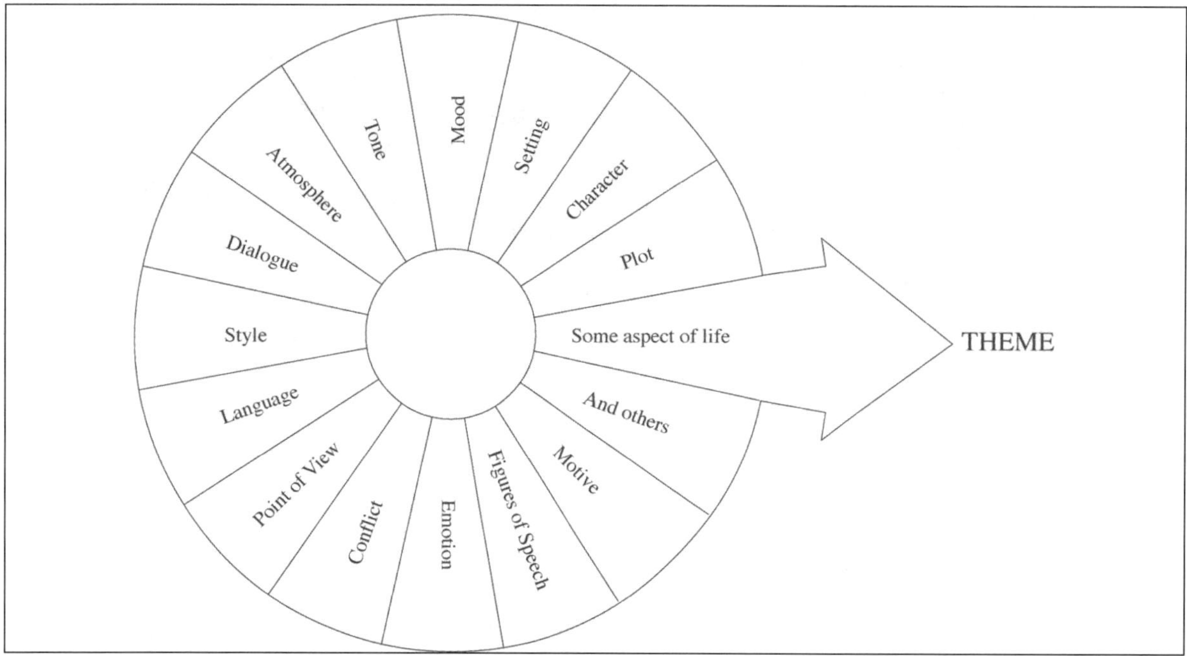

The moral of a story and its theme are connected, but they are not the same. A **moral** is a conclusion drawn from events in a story; it is a statement about the best way to behave. If a story has a moral (not all do), then sometimes the author states it. It is more common for the moral to be left for the reader to discover.

Poetry

A **poem** is piece of writing that presents vivid experiences, ideas, or emotions by appealing to the imagination of the reader. Poems produce their effect through the use of images, sounds, and rhythm. They frequently contain poetic devices, such **alliteration** and **onomatopoeia** (two sound-devices), and figures of speech, such as **metaphor** and **simile** (two ways of making comparisons). Poems often contain **allusions**, or indirect mention of things such as other literature or history.

All of these characteristics can make poetry more challenging to read, and for some, difficult to understand. However, poetry can be rewarding—there is a reason many people, and not just poets, write poems to express themselves in moments of grief or triumph. Think of the heartfelt poems written for a funeral or for graduation.

Since a poem is so densely packed with layers of meaning and poetic techniques, reading poetry is an exercise in unpacking the layers. Here is a way of reading a poem that you may find helpful.

- **Read a poem more than once, each time paying attention to a different level of meaning.**

- **First, try to understand the words themselves, then the imagery, then the symbols, then the allusions, and then the poetic techniques.**

- **Finally, the meaning of the entire poem should be easier to understand and appreciate.**

Here is an outline of the method.

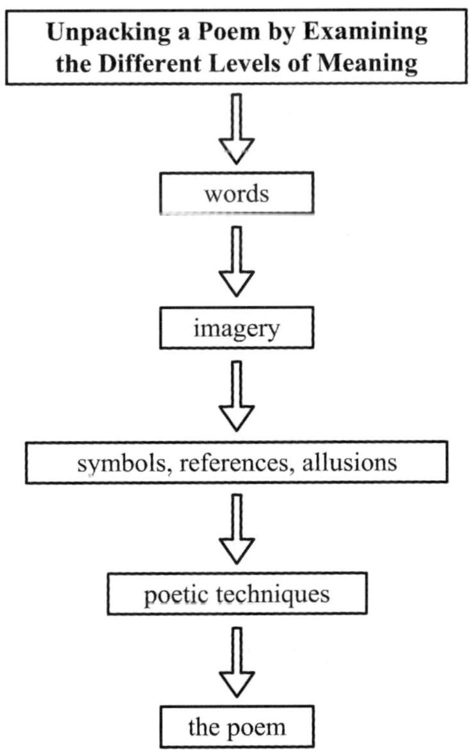

⚷   **You might find that understanding the words and understanding the imagery go together. Or, you might find that the order of understanding is different for different poems—or for different readers. That is to be expected. This way of reading a poem is a suggestion, not a prescription. Use the method or adapt it, to meet your needs.**

Here is an example of reading of a poem using this method. The poem is written by Marjorie Pickthall (1883-1922), an English and Canadian poet and writer.

Stars

Now in the West the slender moon lies low,
And now Orion glimmers through the trees,
Clearing the earth with even pace and slow,
And now the stately-moving Pleiades,
5   In that soft infinite darkness overhead
Hang jewel-wise upon a silver thread.

And all the lonelier stars that have their place,
Calm lamps within the distant southern sky,
And planet-dust upon the edge of space,
10   Look down upon the fretful world, and I
Look up to outer vastness unafraid
And see the stars which sang when earth was made.

Understanding the Words

Understanding the meaning of each word is the first step in understanding the whole poem. Here are the words that might need to be looked up—or at least noticed and thought about.

the West	West is a compass direction; when capitalized, it represents a region
slender moon	Crescent moon: the moon is either waxing or waning
glimmer	Give a faint, intermittent light
stately	Impressive, dignified, and graceful
pace	Speed of walking or running, or other movement
Orion, the Pleiades	Two constellations, or groups of stars often named after characters from Greek mythology; Orion was a hunter, and the Pleiades were seven sisters
-wise	In a certain way, direction, or manner
jewel-wise	In the way that a jewel does
planet-dust	Vast dust clouds in space are compressed by gravity to form planets and stars
edge of space	Since the time of the ancient Greeks, astronomers have known that the universe is vast; until the 1920s and the discovery of galaxies, no one knew quite *how* vast; *the edge of space* might be figure of speech, or it might be meant to be accurate according to the knowledge of the time
fretful	Agitated, disturbed

Understanding the Imagery

The author's emotional response to the night sky (and to all of life) is carefully developed through a series of images. She looks up at the night sky and she sees the moon and stars.

slender moon lies low	The crescent moon is setting
Orion glimmers through the trees	The stars are seen through branches: the leaves must have fallen; it is fall or winter
clears the earth	The constellation is rising in the east
overhead	The Pleiades rise before Orion and are high in the sky; the placement of the moon and stars are correct for a night in November in the early 1900s
jewel-wise upon a silver thread	The jewels are compared to a necklace; thread is an allusion to star charts that show the stars connected with lines; the entire image recalls the beauty of diamonds and silver

The night sky is **personified**, or given human characteristics. Words like *slender, even pace, stately-moving, lonelier, calm,* and *look down* all make the heavenly bodies appear to be alive and aware. The images are all beautiful and peaceful: *the Pleiades, / In that soft infinite darkness overhead / Hang jewel-wise upon a silver thread.*

Understanding the Symbols, References, and Allusions

Poetry often includes elements that refer to things other than themselves.

A **symbol** is something that stands for something else, especially for something abstract. In this poem, the stars are symbols of peace, order, and purpose.

A **reference** is a direct mention of something that is related to whatever is being discussed. The mention of *Romeo and Juliet* at the beginning of this *KEY* is an example. However, the images and references in this poem are indirect.

An **allusion** is an indirect reference. Because they are indirect, allusions can be more difficult to recognize and to understand. Writers and poets often expect their readers to have certain knowledge or to be familiar with certain events or writings. References and allusions often refer to historical, mythological, and religious subjects.

Line 1 may contain an allusion to the World War I slang to *go west*, which means *to die*. The term itself is an allusion to the death toll on the Western Front. If the moon is *waning* (becoming less), then *slender moon* would support this interpretation. The moon is certainly setting, which does support the interpretation. All this accounts for the capitalization of *west*, a word that is not capitalized when used as a direction.

Lines 10 and 11 contain an allusion to Pascal's[1] famous words about the vastness of space: *The eternal silence of these infinite spaces terrifies me.* Rosemary Pickthall, however, feels the opposite: *I look up to outer vastness unafraid.*

Line 12 is an allusion to the Book of Job from the Bible, when God speaks to Job about the creation of the earth, *When the morning stars sang together, and all the sons of God shouted for joy.*[2] Job, like the *fretful world* (line 10) had suffered greatly, and this line about the creation of the world is part of the response to his suffering.

This poem was published **posthumously** (after the author's death) in 1925. Depending on when she wrote (or last worked on) the poem, *the West* (line 1) may be a symbol of death.

---

[1] *Blaise Pascal (1623-1662)*—French mathematician, scientist, and religious philosopher. The line is from his *Pensées.*
[2] *sons of God (Job 38:7)*—angels, heavenly powers

Understanding the Poetic Techniques

A **lyric** is a short poem expressing personal thoughts and feelings—clearly, "Stars" is a lyric poem.

"Stars" is divided into two sections, or **stanzas**, like paragraphs. Stanzas have the same function as paragraphs. Notice that the first stanza is a description of what the writer sees in the night sky, while the second is a description of her reaction to what she sees. The poem has a regular rhyme scheme. In each **stanza**, or group of verses, the last words of each **verse**, or line of poetry, rhymes in an **ababcc** pattern. The regularity of the rhyme scheme matches the regular movement of the stars in the night sky.

Lines 1–4 and 7–9 are all **end-stopped**; they end with a comma that indicates a pause. Lines 5, 10, and 11, however, have no end punctuation. The thought continues without a pause into the next line. This technique, called **enjambment**, varies the rhythm of the poem to avoid monotony and it emphasizes the enjambed lines. In this poem, the enjambment is used at the end of each stanza to emphasize the most important idea; it also varies the regular rhythm.

"Stars" is written with a regular rhythm; it is an example of **metrical**, or traditional poetry.

Metrical or Traditional Poetry

Not all poetry rhymes, but nearly all poetry has strong rhythm. Finding that rhythm will allow you to read the poem as the author intended it to be read, and the rhythm will often provide clues to meaning. This is especially true if the poet has used irregular **syntax** (sentence structure) or complicated imagery.

The basic of rhythm in metrical poetry should be understood. First, recall how a dictionary shows words divided into syllables. The stressed syllables are marked with accents: *re·mem′·ber, com′·men·tar′·y.*[3] In metrical poetry, the regular alternation of stressed and unstressed syllables produces the regular rhythm. The rhythm of poetry is called **meter**[4] and a unit of rhythm is called a **foot**. Certain metrical feet have names. Two of the most common are:

> *iambic foot: unstressed, **stressed** (today, abstain, the **right**)*
>
> *trochaic foot: **stressed**, unstressed (**counter, chemist, once upon a midnight**)*

A line of metrical poetry is usually made up of a fixed number of feet. A poem written in **iambic pentameter**, the most common meter in English-language metrical poetry, has lines of five **iambs**. (*Penta* is Greek for five and an iamb has two syllables. The average line has ten syllables).

Poets pattern words into a regular rhythm that can be indicated with stress marks above syllables:

> *"—" above an <u>unaccented</u> syllable (weak stress)"*
>
> *" / " above an <u>accented</u> syllable (strong stress).*

---

[3] The second example has primary and secondary stress. Both may be regarded simply as stressed syllables.
[4] *meter/metre*—in Canada, use *meter* for the rhythm of poetry and use *metre* for the unit of measure.

This kind of careful examination of the rhythm of a poem is called **scansion**. Here is the first stanza, **scanned**.

	—	/	—	/	—	/	—	/	—	/
1	Now	in	the	West	the	slen	der	moon	lies	low,
	—	/	—	/	—	/	—	/	—	/
2	And	now	O	ri	on	glim	mers	through	the	trees,
	/	—	—	/	—	/	—	/	—	/
3	Clear	ing	the	earth	with	e	ven	pace	and	slow,
	—	/	—	/	—	/	—	/	—	/
4	And	now	the	state	ly	-mov	ing	Ple	ia	des,
	—	/	—	/	—	/	—	/	—	/
5	In	that	soft	in	finite*	dark	ness	o	ver	head
	—	/	—	/	—	/	—	/	—	/
6	Hang	jew	el	-wise	up	on	a	sil	ver	thread.

Notice that line 3 begins with a trochee, not an iamb. Iambic pentameter is very forgiving of slight variations. In fact, poets often deliberately add slight variations to avoid monotony. This poem is written in iambic pentameter. Also notice that in line 5, *infinite* is best pronounced as though it has (almost) two syllables. This preserves the most common meter and the number of syllables per line.

The regularity of the rhyme scheme and the regular number of syllables in each line match the regular movement of the stars in the night sky.

Understanding the Poem as a Whole

At this point, the work of understanding the poem should be a matter of summarizing the main points of the analysis. The poem is a **lyric**, a short poem that expresses the emotions or thoughts of the writer. The first stanza describes the night sky and the second stanza describes the poet's thoughts about life. Both stanzas express her emotions.

Free Verse and Rhythm

Free verse also contains rhythm although it is not as regular. Here is a short poem by Walt Whitman. Try reading it aloud. Notice the definite, but irregular, rhythm. This kind of rhythm is sometimes called cadence, and it is closer to ordinary speech than the regular rhythms of metrical verse are.

When I Heard the Learn'd Astronomer

When I heard the learn'd astronomer,
When the proofs, the figures, were ranged in columns before me,
When I was shown the charts and diagrams, to add, divide, and measure them,
4   When I sitting heard the astronomer where he lectured with much applause in the
                                               lecture-room,
How soon unaccountable I became tired and sick,
Till rising and gliding out I wander'd off by myself,
In the mystical moist night-air, and from time to time,
8   Look'd up in perfect silence at the stars.

Notice how Whitman turns the two-syllable *learned*[5] into the one-syllable *learn'd*. In writing free verse, he is just as careful with rhythm as a poet writing metrical verse, only his rhythms are different. When reading free verse, read with the rhythm and listen to how it contributes to the poet's intention. In this example, lines 3–5 are long and written with a repetitive rhythm that echoes Whitman's boredom and dislike. The rhythms of the concluding lines change as he escapes from the lecture-room.

Kinds of Poetry

The Sonnet

The sonnet is a complex form that has been popular for centuries. **Sonnets** are lyric poems fourteen lines long, and when written in English, usually iambic pentameter. The **Elizabethan,** or **Shakespearean** sonnet consists of three **quatrains** (four-line stanzas) and a **couplet** (two lines) all written to a strict **end-rhyme scheme** (*abab cdcd efef gg*). The development of the poet's thoughts is also structured. There are several methods; one method is to use each quatrain for different points in an argument and the couplet for the resolution of the argument. Because of the complexity of the sonnet, poets sometimes find it a suitable form for expressing the complexity of thought and emotion.

---

[5] *learned*—when *learned* is used as an adjective, it is pronounced with two syllables: *learn-ed*. Whitman's *learn'd* is pronounced like the verb.

Genre

Lyric	A short poem that expresses the emotions or thoughts of the writer. Sonnets, odes, and elegies are examples of lyrics. (*Lyrics* are the words of a song. A song is often a lyric in the first sense.)
Ode	A poem expressing lofty emotion. Odes often celebrate an event, or are addressed to nature or to some person, place, or thing. An example is "Ode to a Grecian Urn" by John Keats.
Ballad	A narrative poem that tells a story, often in a straightforward and dramatic manner, and often about such universals as love, honour, and courage. Ballads were once songs. Literary ballads often have the strong rhythm and plain rhymes of songs. (Songs are still written in ballad form, some old ballads are still sung, and some literary ballads have been set to music.) Samuel Taylor Coleridge's "The Rime of the Ancient Mariner" is an example of a literary ballad. "The Mary Ellen Carter" by Stan Rogers is an example of a modern song-ballad.
Epic	A long poem that is often about a heroic character. The style is elevated and the poetry often represents religious, or cultural ideals. The *Iliad* and the *Odyssey* are examples of epics.

☞ **Each of these kinds of poems could be written as free verse or in any of the traditional meters.**

Poetic Devices

Poetic devices are the tools that poets use to convey emotion and meaning. Here are some of the more common devices.

Alliteration	The repetition of initial consonants. *Lo, praise of the prowess of people-kings / of spear-armed Danes, in days long sped . . .*[6]
Assonance	Like rhyme, but only the repeated vowels are the same or almost the same. (*load, loan; mess, lend*). Another kind of assonance is called half rhyme. Consonants match, but vowels do not (*tin, tan; stake, stick*). Some poems use half rhyme in place of full rhyme.
Dissonance	The use of discordant or unpleasant sounds.
Onomatopoeia	The use of words that suggest the sound of the thing they describe. Tennyson's *murmuring of innumerable bees* imitates the sound of bees through the use of assonance.

---

[6] From *Beowulf.*

Rhyme	The repetition of the same sounds. Syllables, entire words, or groups of words can rhyme. As a rule, rhyme consists of the last stressed vowel and all the sounds after it. (*infernal, eternal; laughter, rafter; ring high; sing high*). Rhyme is usually found at the end of a line of poetry, but sometimes it occurs within the line (internal rhyme).
Simile	A comparison using *like* or *as*: *an eager spirit like a bright flame.*
Apostrophe[7]	A figure of speech addressed to someone who is dead or absent, or to an inanimate object. (See personification.)
Metonymy	A figure of speech that uses an attribute of a thing or something associated with the thing to stand for the thing itself. *The **suits** make the decisions around here.*
Synecdoche	Like metonymy except that a part of something is used to stand for the whole thing. *Many **hands** make light work.*
Personification	The attribution of human characteristics to non-human things. Shakespeare's *Blow, blow, thou winter wind, / Thou art not so unkind / As man's ingratitude; / Thy tooth is not so keen* contains both an apostrophe and personification.
Symbolism	The use of one thing to represent something else. Although symbolism is similar to metonymy, the association may be arbitrary (a maple leaf has nothing to do with Canada as a country, and the maple tree grows in many countries), or else the symbolism may be invented by the author.

Read poetic language with careful attention. For example, *leaves whispering* may be intended **literally**, for trees in a poem may be aware and have the power of speech. However, the words are more likely meant **figuratively**. Then how are they to be understood? A metaphor like *leaves whispering* can have several functions.

- It can describe the *sound* of moving leaves by comparing them to whispering.

- It can also describe something else—perhaps a voice—by comparing it to the sound of moving leaves: *a small voice like dry leaves whispering*.

- The same figure of speech can be used to suggest something other than just sound; for example, the whispering leaves could represent nature communicating secrets impossible to hear.

In the last case, the metaphor would be an important part of the poet's thought and it might be developed at length, or it might appear again in other parts of the poem. An extended metaphor, especially if it is elaborate, is called a **conceit**.

---

[7] Do not confuse this apostrophe with the punctuation mark (')

Writing Essays

An Essay Template

Many students find essay writing very challenging. This partly because they do not realize that there is a pattern to the basic essay, and that the pattern can be easily learned and applied.

- **This pattern is based on graphic organizers. It is intended to be a starting point for most of the essays that you will have to write. Naturally, you will alter the basic pattern to suit your own abilities and tastes.**

Begin with the familiar **hamburger paragraph**, which looks like this:

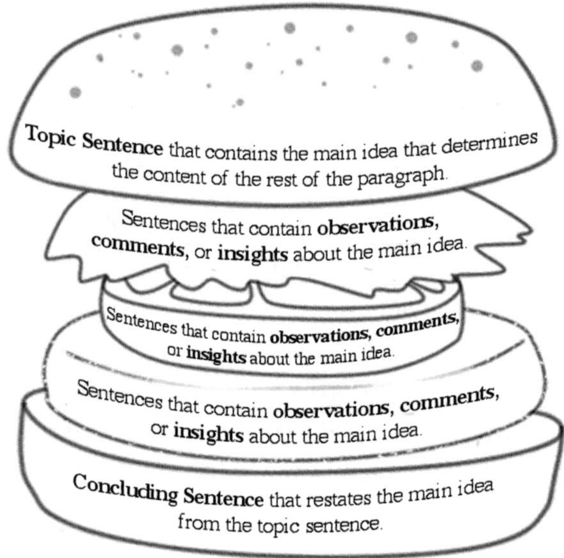

Begin with a topic sentence that introduces the controlling idea of the paragraph.

Write several sentences that develop the idea introduced in the first sentence. These sentences contain observations, comments, or insights about the main idea. In these sentences, you might also present supporting details, listing evidence or examples, tell an anecdote, give an explanation, or advance an argument.

End with a concluding sentence that restates the controlling idea.

Now, consider the whole essay. Think about another hamburger:

Introductory paragraph that introduces the **Controlling Idea** or **Thesis Statement**.

Paragraph that contains **Supporting Details** about one aspect of the controlling idea.

Paragraph that contains **Supporting Details** about one aspect of the controlling idea.

Paragraph that contains **Supporting Details** about one aspect of the controlling idea.

Concluding Paragraph that sums up the ideas or restates the thesis in a more interesting way.

Begin with an introductory paragraph that introduces the controlling idea of the essay. This paragraph is also used to capture the reader's interest, suggest an overall order for your essay, and indicate your position relative to the controlling idea. The introductory paragraph often concludes with the thesis statement.

Write several paragraphs in which you develop the controlling idea that you introduced in the introductory paragraph. Each paragraph should contain supporting details, explanations, or arguments related to one aspect of the controlling idea.

End with a concluding paragraph that restates the controlling idea or that sums up the whole essay in a different way.

- Use the hamburger structure as a mental image, sketch it on paper, or translate the image into a simple written list.

- Remember that every sentence in a paragraph should relate to the topic sentence, and each sentence and paragraph should relate to the controlling idea of the essay.

Present the content of your essay in a logical order.

- Order is often reinforced by the use of transitional words or phrases such as 'in addition', 'as a result', 'for example', and 'on the other hand'.

- Instructions are usually written in the order in which they are to be carried out.

- Narratives are often told in chronological order, from the first event to the last.

- Arguments may be structured in order of importance from the least important to most important or from most important to least important.

- For a compare-and-contrast essay, in the first paragraph of the body, you might discuss similarities. In the second paragraph, differences, and in the third, the significance of the similarities and differences.

- Another logical way of organizing compare-and-contrast essay is to start with a paragraph in which you discuss a similarity and its significance. In the next paragraph, you might discuss a difference and its significance, and in the third paragraph discuss another similarity and its significance, and so on.

- Yet another way to organize such an essay is to start with a paragraph in which you discuss a similarity, a related difference, and their significance. In the next paragraph, you would discuss another similarity, a related difference, and their significance, and so on.

- In a defend-a-position essay, after your introductory paragraph, you might start with a paragraph in which you summarize the main facts about a problem. In the next paragraph, you might examine opposing points of view. These could be followed by a paragraph in which you introduce and defend a position and a paragraph in which you address possible objections to the position.

In each of the paragraphs develop one aspect of the thesis statement. Use these paragraphs to clarify and support your thesis statement by

- explaining, arguing, or defending

- listing evidence or giving examples

- comparing and contrasting

- describing, analyzing, or summarizing

- making observations

- detailing your thoughts and ideas

- expressing insights about the topic

- using short, appropriate quotations

Remember that the controlling idea not only controls the choice of supporting details, it also controls the organization and such things as the choice of suitable words and phrases.

The Thesis Statement

It is not absolutely necessary to include a thesis statement in the first paragraph; in fact, it is not always necessary to actually state a thesis. Sometimes a thesis is implied. However, many teachers like to see the thesis statement laid out plainly in the first paragraph.

The thesis is the same thing as the theme. The **thesis** is made up of a topic and a point of view. It is often called the **controlling idea** because it is the idea that controls the selection of all the other ideas included in the essay.

$$\boxed{\text{Thesis}} = \boxed{\text{Theme}} = \boxed{\text{Controlling Idea}}$$

A **thesis statement** is a sentence that expresses the thesis. The thesis statement includes the topic and what will be said about the topic.

$$\boxed{\text{Macbeth}} + \boxed{\text{is destroyed by his ambition}} = \boxed{\text{Thesis Statement}}$$

⚷ The thesis statement is often a single sentence.

The hamburger paragraph can be used to include the thesis statement. Here is a template for the first paragraph.

1	Write a topic sentence that introduces the topic itself.
2	Write several sentences that explain the topic.
3	Write a thesis statement that restates the topic and *tells what position you will be taking.*

Transitional Devices

Transitional devices are words and phrases like *because, also, in addition, nevertheless,* and *as a result.* These words show the relationship between ideas.

> ***In addition,*** *the witness has already admitted to lying.* ***Therefore,*** *you must consider whether or not any of her evidence can be believed.* ***On the other hand,*** *other witnesses have confirmed some of her statements.*

Careful writers use transitional devices to make the relationships between the parts of an essay clear. Transitional devices can be used to show a sequence or to begin a paragraph by showing how the ideas in the paragraph are related to the ideas in the preceding paragraph.

> *As you consider the evidence, you will have to keep in mind the fact that the witness has admitted to lying on three occasions.* ***First,*** *. . . .* ***Next,*** *. . .* ***And finally,*** *. . . .*
>
> ***On the other hand,*** *her evidence about the escape vehicle has been confirmed by . . . .* ***Therefore,*** *you will have to decide how much weight to give to her statements about . . . .*
>
> *To conclude, it seems that we can agree . . . .Detecting Logical Fallacies*

Essays are often meant to persuade. Sometimes persuasion is based on appeals to emotion, but the only lasting persuasion is based on facts and reason. Facts can be difficult to check, but the logical presentation of facts can be checked by anyone who is prepared to pay attention to detail and to use common sense.

You have to know some history to know that the following sentence is nonsense.

> *Once Grand Duchess Amelia had been crowned queen-empress of Transylvania, she immediately began to plot the invasion of France.*

However, you can easily see that the following is nonsense.

> *Well of course he's crooked. He's a politician, isn't he? And we know what politicians are like.*

A moment's thought makes it clear that there is no way that we can conclude anything about people's honesty from the mere fact that they are politician. We can easily see the error in thought if the statements are rearranged and written in the form of a syllogism:

All politicians are corrupt.	*major premise*	*All P are C*
He is a politician.	*minor premise*	*X is P*
He is corrupt.	*conclusion*	*X is C*

We can see that the conclusion follows, *but only if both premises are true.* In other words, the argument is valid, *but only if all politicians are corrupt.* How can we possibly know that for a fact? We know enough about human nature to doubt that premise. There is no reason why any individual might not be honest. Simply taking up a certain profession does not automatically produce corruption.

Syllogisms allow you to examine statements and decide if the logical connections between them are valid. Although you cannot check matters of fact with a syllogism, you can check matters of logic. Then you can easily discover the facts that you need to check through investigation. Here is an example.

> *Recently, a wild game farm was closed after it was discovered that the animals on the farm were starving. An animal rights activist was interviewed on television and said, among other things, "This is the second time this has happened. Enough is enough. This is a failed experiment and the government must shut down all wild game farms."*

The activist might have been right or he might have been wrong, but his argument was inadequate. He said two things:

1	*More than one failed game farm shows that all game farms have failed.*
	Two game farms have failed.
	All game farms are a failure.
2	*If all game farms are a failure, they should be closed.*
	All game farms are a failure.
	All game farms should be closed.

The activist's conclusions follow, *but only if his premises were true.* Of course, we have no way of knowing that. They premises might be true, or they might not be. Further investigation is required.

Sometimes the syllogism itself is invalid. In this example, conclusion does not follow from the premises.

All mammals are warm-blooded.	*major premise*	*All M are W*
Birds are not mammals.	*minor premise*	*B are not M*
Birds are not warm-blooded.	*conclusion*	*B are not W*

This argument is invalid. The major premise is about M and W, the conclusion is about B and W, but the minor premise is about B and M. *There is nothing to connect B and W.*

The conclusion is also false. We know that birds are warm-blooded.

☞ **Use syllogisms to analyze arguments.**

☞ **Remember that syllogisms cannot be used to check matters of fact.**

☞ **If a premise is false, then the conclusion does not follow, but that conclusion might still be a true statement. It is just that the argument needs to be improved.**

☞ **Remember that if an argument is invalid, then the conclusion does not follow, *but that conclusion might still be true statement.* It is just that the argument needs to be improved.**

Grammar

Parts of Speech

1. **Nouns** are the names of persons, places, or things.

- **Countable** nouns like marbles, trees, and stars that can be counted and may be singular or plural.
- **Uncountable** nouns like *maturity, intelligence,* and *courage* cannot be counted and are singular.
- Nouns like *water, sand,* and *grain* are countable or uncountable depending on their use.
- **Collective** nouns like *committee, staff, family, crowd,* and *class* are singular unless there is a particular reason to treat them as plural.
- **Nominals** are words or phrases used as nouns. *Skiing, watching paint dry,* and *to go long distance running* are not nouns, but they could be used as nouns in some sentences.
- **Appositives** are words or phrases that rename a noun. *My friend Jack will be there.* (*Jack,* an appositive, renames *friend.*)
- **Proper nouns** are names of particular things and must be capitalized.

2. **Pronouns** take the place of nouns.

- The **antecedent** of a pronoun is the noun that the pronoun stands for. In *Goneril demanded that she be first*, the antecedent of *she* is *Goneril*.

- **Indefinite** pronouns like *all, another, anybody, somebody, nobody,* and *none* are generally singular.

3. **Adjectives** modify, or describe, nouns and pronouns.

- **Adjectivals** are any word or group of words that act as adjectives.

- The **articles**, *a, an,* and *the,* are considered adjectives.

- Capitalize **proper adjectives** unless long use has made them **common.** (*Canadian, Parisian,* but *italic (script), gothic (novel), zeppelin*)

4. **Verbs** usually name actions: *laugh, sleep, think.*

- Most English verbs are **regular**; that is, their past tense and past participle forms end in *-ed*. There are about three hundred **irregular** verbs, but not all are in common use. Reference texts contain lists of irregular verbs.

- **Transitive** verbs have a direct object. They do something to the object.

    The ball struck the batter. Batter is the direct object of *struck.*

- **Intransitive** verbs do not have direct objects. The verbs *lie* (to tell a lie) and *arrive* are intransitive. You cannot *arrive* anything, or *lie* anything.

- Most verbs are transitive or intransitive depending on how they are used.

    Transitive: *He produced a sheaf of papers.*

    Intransitive: *When irrigated, the wasteland produced abundantly.*

- **Linking** verbs like *be, taste, look,* and *sound* describe states of being. Other linking verbs like *turn, become,* and *grow* describe changes in state. Linking verbs are usually followed by nouns or adjectives (that is, nominals or adjectivals).

    She is a *lawyer.*

    This *milk* tastes *sour.*

5. **Adverbs** modify, or describe, a verb, an adjective, or another adverb.

    She ran *quickly.*

    His *closely* reasoned argument was brilliant.

    They worked *very* hard.

- **Adverbials** are any word or group of words that act as an adverb.

    After the long, hard day, we went fishing.

- Adverbs and adverbials describe **when, where, how, why,** and **how much.**

    You can rest *later.*

    She went *somewhere over the rainbow.*

    They shuffled their feet *nervously.*

    Because he was sick, he fell down.

    I can't believe you ate *all of it.*

6. **Prepositions** are words placed in front of nouns and pronouns.

   > *For* a cause
   >
   > *By* them

- Together with the noun or pronoun, prepositions modify, or describe, some other word in the sentence.

  > They worked *for a cause. For a cause* is an adverbial prepositional phrase modifying *worked*.
  >
  > The child *by them* shouted. *By them* is an adjectival prepositional phrase modifying *child*.

- **Prepositional phrases** are usually adjectivals or adverbials.

7. **Conjunctions** join words, phrases, clauses, and sentences. They also show the relationship between the things that are joined. They show whether the things joined are equal or unequal.

- Conjunctions connect both sentences and sentence parts.

- **Coordinating** conjunctions like *and, so,* and *or* join equal parts.

  > Sir Toby likes *cakes* **and** *ale.*
  >
  > You must *lead* **or** *follow.*
  >
  > *Chopping firewood* **and** *painting the trim* are next.
  >
  > *We went to the wedding,* **and** *we went to the reception.*

- **Correlative** conjunctions like *either-or* and *neither-nor* join equal parts.

  > Malvolio likes **neither** *cakes* **nor** ale.
  >
  > You must either *lead* **or** *follow.*
  >
  > **Either** *you must chop firewood,* **or** *you must paint the trim.*

- **Subordinating** conjunctions like *whenever* and *however* join unequal parts.

  > **Whenever** *I hear that song,* I want to laugh.
  >
  > You must be careful **whenever** *you cross the street.*
  >
  > **However** *you arrange it,* be sure that you are back by Tuesday.

8. **Interjections** express some form of emotion.

   > *Ouch*! That hurts
   >
   > *Oh*, I don't know.

The Sentence

Sentences are made up of **subject** and **predicate**. The minimum subject is a noun and the minimum predicate is a verb. When proofreading and editing, it is often necessary to focus on the minimum subject and predicate.

Subject			Predicate		
nominal	+	everything attached to the nominal	**verb**	+	everything attached to the verb
Birds			**fly**.		
The **suspects**			**are** the ones.		
The five **suspects** that you see before you this morning			**are** certainly the ones who raided the fridge during the night.		

Sometimes the subject comes after predicate.

Predicate	Subject
Down the mountainside **thundered**	the **avalanche**.

Sentence Faults

Lack of Agreement Among Parts of a Sentence

1.   Subject and Verb

The basic rule of subject-verb agreement should not cause any difficulty.

> *It **is** ready.*
>
> *They **are** ready.*
>
> *Sampson and Delilah **are** not friends any more.*

Most of the difficulties in subject-verb agreement are caused by difficulties in recognizing singular and plural subjects.

> i)   When subjects joined by **or** or **nor,** the verb agrees with the nearest subject.
>
> > *Either Miller **or** Smith **is** guilty.*
> >
> > *Neither Miller **nor** Smith **wants** to confess.*
> >
> > *Neither the **speaker** nor the **listeners** are aware of the irony.*
>
> When one part of the verb is singular, and the other plural, write the sentence so that the plural part is nearest the verb.
>
> > Weak: *Neither **band members** nor the conductor **is** satisfied.*
> >
> > Better: *Neither the **conductor** nor the **band members** are satisfied.*

ii) Nothing that comes between a singular subject and its verb can make that subject plural. In other words, do not make the verb agree with the nearest noun.

> Our school basketball **team**, *the Gerbils*, **is** *victorious again.*
>
> The **prime minister**, *accompanied by several cabinet ministers,* **arrives** *at the airport shortly.*
>
> Either **Miller** *or* **Jones**—*both are suspects*—**is** *guilty.*
>
> The **contestant** *with the most votes* **is** *now on the stage.*
>
> **One** *of the girls* **sings** *better.*
>
> The **ringleader** *who was at the head of the rebellious miners* **is** *sorry.*

iii) Indefinite pronouns like *each, each one, either, neither, everyone, everybody, anybody, anyone, nobody, somebody, someone,* and *no one* are singular.

> **Each** *of contestants* **wins** *a prize.*
>
> **Everybody** *near the river* **is** *in danger.*
>
> **No one** *who wants to be successful in these exams* **is** *likely to be late.*

iv) Collective nouns are singular unless there is a reason to consider them as plurals.

> The **group works** *well.*
>
> The **company is** *bankrupt.*
>
> The **jury is** *deliberating its verdict.*
>
> The **jury are** *arguing among themselves.*

2. The Wrong Pronoun

Using the correct pronoun is often a problem because the form of a pronoun varies depending on how the pronoun is used.

i) Use *I, you, he/she/it, we, you, they, who,* as the subject of a sentence or clause, and for the complement of a linking verb.

> **You** *have been chosen.*
>
> **We** *will be the last of the contestants.*
>
> **Who** *is going to be next?*
>
> *It is* **she** *who will be chosen.*

ii) Use *me, you, him/her/it, us, you, them,* and *whom* as direct or indirect objects of verbs or as the object of a preposition.

> *Give it to* **me**.
>
> *Hit the ball to* **them**.
>
> *Ask* **them** *the time.*
>
> *The child next to* **him** *laughed suddenly.*

iii)   Use *my, your, his/her/its, our, your, their,* and *whose* as adjectives.

> ***my*** *car*
>
> ***your*** *umbrella*
>
> ***its*** *fur*

iv)   Use *mine, yours, his/hers/its, ours, yours, theirs,* and *whose* as subjects of sentences or as the complement of a linking verb.

> ***Yours*** *is the one on the left.*
>
> *This is* ***mine****.*
>
> ***Theirs*** *is next.*

☞   **The possessive pronouns—my, your, his, hers, its, our, yours, theirs, and whose— NEVER use an apostrophe to show possession.**

3. Fragments, Comma Splices, and Run-ons

As a general rule, all sentences should be complete sentences.

> Incorrect: *He went ahead with his plan. <u>Even though it was faulty.</u>*
>
> Correct: *He went ahead with his plan, even though it was faulty.*

Occasionally, an incomplete sentence can be used deliberately. Such **minor sentences** are used for effect.

> Correct: *Is anyone is in favour of dictatorship? <u>No</u>? <u>Well, of course not.</u>*

Of course, dialogue and reported speech are exceptions to the rule about fragments.

> *"Ready yet?"*
>
> *"Not yet."*
>
> *"Well then—!"*

The opposite error is the "sentence" that is really two sentences. Either punctuation between sentences is omitted, or a comma is used to join two sentences.

> Run-on: *We went to Calgary we decided to visit Banff.*
>
> Comma splice: *We went to Calgary, we decided to visit Banff.*

These errors can be fixed by correcting the punctuation or by rewriting.

> *We went to Calgary. We decided to visit Banff.*
>
> *We went to Calgary. Then we decided to visit Banff.*
>
> *After we went to Calgary, we decided to visit Banff.*
>
> *We went to Calgary; then we decided to visit Banff.*

Punctuation

1. Periods

The period is used at the end of most sentences and after fragments[8] that are deliberately used as sentences.

> *I walked to the end of the world. And stared.*

Do not use a period after a complete sentence that is contained by parentheses within another sentence.

> *Afghanistan is making progress (seven thousand technicians have been trained) and will one day finish the job of clearing mines.*

2. Punctuating Possessives

Most possessives are formed by adding an apostrophe and an *–s*.

> *a girl's smile*
>
> *one country's history*

The possessive of nouns ending in an *–s* sound is formed by adding an apostrophe and an *–s*.

> *the boss's car*
>
> *Charles's, Alex's*

The possessive of plurals is formed by adding an apostrophe after the *–s* of the plural.

> *five girls' smiles*
>
> *three countries' histories*

3. Commas

a. Commas With Conjunctions

The **coordinating conjunctions** are used to join complete sentences. They are usually followed by a comma. The coordinating conjunctions are *for, and, nor, but, or, yet,* and *so*. They may be remembered by remembering the mnemonic FANBOYS.

> *He will be late, for he must complete the game.*
>
> *Go to the edge of the cliff, and tell me what you see there.*

When a coordinate conjunction joins two short independent clauses, a comma may not be necessary.

> *She's late and she's tired.*

When **subordinating conjunctions** (which include *after, because, although, if, before, since, though,* and *unless*) are used in an introductory clause, a comma follows the clause.

> *Because you have been elected, you must serve.*
>
> *Before she leaves, she plans to write a note of farewell.*

Do not use a semicolon to follow an introductory clause.

> Incorrect*: Because you have been elected; you must serve.*

---

[8] To avoid confusion, fragments that are used deliberately are sometimes called **minor sentences**.

When the subordinate clause follows the independent clause, a comma is usually not used.

She plans to write a note of farewell before she leaves.

You must serve because you have been elected.

However, a comma should be used when it is necessary to avoid confusion.

Unclear: *He has done all his work since his failure last term threatened his final grade.*

Clear: *He has done all his work, since his failure last term threatened his final grade.*

Until near the end, the original sentence seems to mean that he has done all his work from the time that his failure threatened his final grade. A comma after work makes it clear that *since* is a subordinating conjunction meaning *because* and not a preposition.

b. Commas With Introductory Phrases

Some introductory phrases have been mentioned previously. Other kinds of introductory phrases are also followed by a comma.

During the long summer afternoon, we were able to catch up on our work.

Knowing he was beaten, he conceded defeat.

Near a small clump of trees, we made our camp.

Running out of money, he cabled home for more.

In addition, we will need rope and flashlights.

When a **conjunctive adverb** (an adverb used as a conjunction) is used after a semicolon, it is still an introductory element.

He had failed his entrance examination; moreover, he had not submitted his papers.

Sometimes a conjunctive adverb does not require a comma. A comma would interrupt the flow of a sentence like the following.

Then we decided to visit Banff.

c. The Serial Comma

Use a comma after all the items in a series.

Bring food, extra clothing, a first aid kit, and matches.

A semicolon should be used after each item in the series when the items already include commas.

The men endured a long, hot march; flies, dust, and brackish water; and a raging, howling sandstorm.

d. Setting Off Appositives

Appositives, or restatements of a **nominal** (a noun, word, or phrase used as a noun) are set off by commas.

> *Our team, the Hornets, is in first place.*
>
> *His American cousins, the Sinclairs, were all present at the reunion.*
>
> *Everyone in Calgary, the home of the Flames hockey team, is watching the Stanley Cup playoffs.*

However, when the appositive is used to distinguish something that belongs to a larger group of similar things, no comma is used.

> *The poem "Stars" was written by Marjorie Pickthall.*
>
> *The Tribal class destroyer HMCS* Athabaskan *was sunk in 1944.*

Notice that HMCS *Athabaskan* cannot rename the noun phrase *Tribal class destroyer*—there were many other ships in that class, or group.

e. Setting Off Nonessential Phrases

Nonessential phrases, which are also called **non-restrictive phrases**, can be removed from a sentence without altering the essential meaning of the sentence. They merely add extra information. Set off nonessential phrases with commas.

> *Her car, which she had painted red, is in the shop again.*
>
> *Her car needs a new transmission, which will be expensive.*

Essential phrases cannot be removed from a sentence without changing the meaning of the sentence. They restrict the meaning of a sentence, and are sometimes called **restrictive phrases**.

> *The car that she needs for work is in the shop again.*

Commas can be used to make a phrase essential or non-essential and thus alter the meaning of a sentence.

> *His uncle, who lives in New York, saw the Trade Towers collapse.*

His uncle saw the collapse. The uncle also happens to live in New York.

> *His uncle who lives in New York saw the Trade Towers collapse.*

One particular uncle saw the collapse. But his other uncles, who live in other cities, did not.

> **Notice that *which* is used with non-essential or non-restrictive phrases. *That* is used with essential or restrictive phrases. *Who* is usually used when referring to persons.**

f. Commas With Adjectives

When more than one adjective appears in front of a noun, commas are sometimes necessary.

> *fierce, tough dogs*
>
> *three fierce, tough dogs*
>
> *three fierce, tough old dogs*
>
> *three fierce old sheep dogs*

Do not put a comma between **cumulative adjectives**, or adjectives that build on each other to modify a noun. Each adjective modifies the noun and adjective group that follows it.

> *four vile yellow plastic figurines*
>
> *her beautiful old Georgian town house*

Cumulative adjectives have a certain order; they cannot be switched around.

> Incorrect*: vile four plastic yellow figurines*
>
> Incorrect*: beautiful her Georgian town old house*

In addition, cumulative adjectives cannot be written with *and*.

> Incorrect*: vile and four and plastic figurines*

The order cannot be changed because there is a conventional order of cumulative adjectives. There are sometimes variations, but this is the most common order.

Article, Possessive, Number	Observation, Judgement, Evaluation, Opinion	Physical Description					Place of Origin, Source	Material, What the Thing is Made Of	Qualifier, Type, Class	Noun
		Size	Shape	Condition	Age	Colour				
several	handsome	big	square	worn	old	red	Italian	leather	running	shoes

Place a comma between **coordinate adjectives**, or adjectives that modify a noun independently. These are often the same kind of adjective.

> *A soft, gentle breeze*
>
> *A harsh, rigid, inflexible critic*

The order of coordinate adjectives can be changed.

> *A gentle, soft breeze*
>
> *A rigid, harsh, inflexible critic*

Notice that *inflexible*, which is used here as an observation or evaluation adjective, is also a physical description adjective. As a result it "sounds" a little better when it is written in the order it would follow if it were used a cumulative adjective describing physical condition.

Coordinate adjectives can also be written with *and*.

> *A soft and gentle breeze*
>
> *A rigid and harsh and inflexible critic*

4. Colons in Sentences

When used in sentences, a colon must follow an independent clause. It introduces a list, an explanation, or an appositive (a word or phrase that restates a noun).

> *You should bring the following items: a sleeping bag, a change of clothes, and matches.*
>
> *There is only one honest thing to do: admit you made a mistake and apologize.*
>
> *His character was summed up in his name: Gradgrind.*

The list may be set up in point form. The same rule applies.

> *The introductory course will cover three topics:*
>
> *1. algebra*
>
> *2. geometry*
>
> *3. trigonometry*

If a list does not follow an independent clause (a complete sentence) no colon is used.

> *You must bring a sleeping bag, a change of clothes, and matches.*
>
> *The introductory course will cover*
>
> *1. algebra*
>
> *2. geometry*
>
> *3. trigonometry*

☞ **A simple way of checking colon use is to cover up all the words after the colon. Can the first part of the sentence now stand alone as a sentence? If not, then do not use the colon.**

> Incorrect: *You must bring: a sleeping bag, a change of clothes, and matches.*
>
> Correct: *You must bring the following items: a sleeping bag, a change of clothes, and matches.*

5. Quotation Marks

Use quotation marks at the beginning and end of all words in a **direct quotation** (someone's exact words). Watch for the use of quotes before and after a speech tag. Also notice the use of the comma after the **speech tag** (*Alfred said*) in the first example.

> *Alfred said, "We are ready."*
>
> *"I'm finished the job," said Alfred. "We can go now."*
>
> *"When we are ready," said Alfred, "we will go."*

Also notice that the closing quotation mark is placed *after* a comma or a period.

Closing quotation marks are also used with exclamation marks and question marks. When these punctuation marks *belong to the sentence*, they are placed *outside* the closing quotation marks.

> *Didn't you hear him say, "I'm in trouble"?*

If the question mark *belongs to the quotation*, it is placed *inside* the quotation marks.

> *He said sadly, "Why is it always me?"*

The same rules apply to end punctuation used for other purposes. Periods and commas belong inside the quotation marks. Exclamation and question marks belong *either* outside *or* inside the quotation marks, depending on whether they belong to the sentence as a whole or to the words inside the quotation marks.

> *You could say that her acting was "over the top."*
>
> *I can't believe that's your "best effort"!*

Indirect quotations, or quotations that do not repeat exact words, never require quotation marks.

> *Alfred asked if we were ready.*
>
> *Alfred said that he had finished the job and that we could go.*

Quotation marks are also used set off the titles of short stories and poems.

> *Marjorie Pickthall wrote "Stars."*

Quotation marks indicate that a word is being used in an unusual sense.

> *"Housekeeping" on the space station is challenging.*

Quotation marks can also show that a word is used **ironically.** (When a word is used ironically, it has a meaning opposite to its literal meaning).

> *The "suicide" of Jan Masaryk marked the end of democracy in Czechoslovakia.*
>
> *It seems that your "help" has put this project three weeks behind.*

READING FOR EXAMINATIONS

When you are reading for an examination, or for any important purpose, you cannot read casually. An overview, a general idea, or a skimming of the main ideas rarely gives the best results. Instead, a **close reading,** a careful examination of everything in a text, is required.

Close Reading

Close reading is like the method of unpacking a poem. (See "Reading Poetry.") It begins with careful attention to the meanings of words and ends with considering the meaning of the entire work.

Close reading is examining the different levels of meaning.

Meanings of words and sentences	• The basic level of understanding what you read is comprehending the meanings of words. A dictionary may be needed. On an exam a dictionary is not available. • Use context clues to figure out, or at least to approximate, the meanings of unfamiliar words.
Meanings of images, symbols, references, allusions	• These literary devices are mostly indirect (references are an exception) but they are important to meaning and must be considered carefully.
Writing techniques	• The most important part of a sentence is often placed first. • The subject of an essay is often stated in the opening paragraph and restated in the last paragraph. The topic of a paragraph is often stated in the first sentence and restated in the last sentence. • Transitional devices guide the development of ideas and they also show the relationships between ideas. • Narratives often follow the structure shown in the plot diagram and contain the elements of narrative described earlier.
The writer's meaning	• The controlling idea (or the theme, or the thesis) controls everything from the form and genre to the choice of words. Consider everything in relation to the controlling idea.

☞   **The multiple-choice questions also require close reading.**

It is just as important to understand the question as it is to understand the text that the question is testing. For example,

> *The reason why the new Globe is so famous could be* **best** *described as*
>
> *A.   it faithfully reproduces so many aspects of the original Globe*
>
> *B.   it has received favourable reviews in the media*
>
> *C.   it has mounted many of Shakespeare's most popular plays*
>
> *D.   Shakespearean drama is timeless*

Questions that contain words like *best, most accurately,* or *most completely* are **evaluation questions**. All the responses are correct to some degree. You need to read the entire question and the relevant part of the text carefully. Then you will be able to choose the *best, most accurate, most complete* answer.

Apply Your Knowledge of Form and Genre

☞ **On an exam, circle or underline important words in your instruction, readings, and questions.**

You know that when you read an essay, there will be an introductory paragraph and a concluding paragraph. It is often useful to read these first. You can also expect to find transitional devices used throughout. You will want to special attention to these devices, perhaps underlining or highlighting them.

On the other hand, a story might be best read in order. You might want to sketch a plot diagram or note characterization, setting, and theme.

Context Clues

You should always pay attention to context. Here is an example that shows why. Suppose you look at the following question.

> *In the context of lines 5–8,* anxious *means*
>
> *A.*   *eager*
>
> *B.*   *worried*
>
> *C.*   *doubtful*
>
> *D.*   *uncertain*

Many students might read the question and immediately choose *worried*—and anxious does mean worried. The other responses are obviously incorrect—but the question refers to lines 5 to 8. *What does the word mean in context?* Reading lines 5 to 8, you find the following sentence.

> *Premier Jones is anxious to read the results of the Cottonwood Developments enquiry as soon as it is available.*

Worried does not fit in the context of the sentence. *Worried to read?* That cannot be right. *Worried* is not used with the preposition *to.* The only word that fits is *eager.* Strictly speaking, such a use is incorrect, but it is common in informal language.

How could you be sure that *anxious* is used to mean *eager*? After all, the word really means *worried.* When you are not sure, read more of the context. Perhaps you might find something like the following.

> *Insider information indicates that the report will completely clear the government of all wrongdoing.*

Now the context of the situation makes the meaning even clearer. Premier Jones would not be *worried* when the report will clear the government. Instead, the premier would be *eager* to read the report.

⚓ **Always pay close attention to context.**

Irony and Levels of Meaning

Students often do poorly when the surface or initial meaning of a text is not the intended or real meaning.

> *It seems that your "help" has put this project three weeks behind.*

In this case, the quotation marks indicate that *help* is meant ironically. **Irony** is the use of words to express something other than the literal meaning. In the following example, Jane Austen is using irony for humorous effect in the opening sentences of *Pride and Prejudice*.

> *It is a truth universally acknowledged that a single man in possession of a good fortune must be in want of a wife.*

When the irony is intended to hurt, and especially when it is accompanied by a cutting tone of voice (or sometimes by quotation marks, as above), it is called **sarcasm**.

In **verbal irony**, the words mean the opposite of their intended meaning. In **situational irony**, there is either a difference between appearance and reality or a difference between what happens and what is expected to happen.

> *It would be ironic if someone died in a car accident on the way to pick up a million dollar lottery win.*
>
> *Irony also exists when a politician defends the rule of law when she is secretly breaking the law.*

The last example is also an example of **hypocrisy**, or doing one thing while saying another.

Dramatic irony and **tragic irony**, are forms of situational irony found in literature. The irony exists when the audience knows something that the characters do no know. Sometimes other characters also know what the audience knows.

> *When King Duncan arrives at Macbeth's castle, he is greeted with a display of hospitality and friendliness. This an example of tragic irony because in the previous scene, Macbeth and Lady Macbeth plotted to murder their king.*

⚓ **Watch for irony of situation or of words. Sometimes the literal meaning is not the intended meaning.**

NOTES

72

NOTES

KEY STRATEGIES

FOR

SUCCESS ON EXAMS

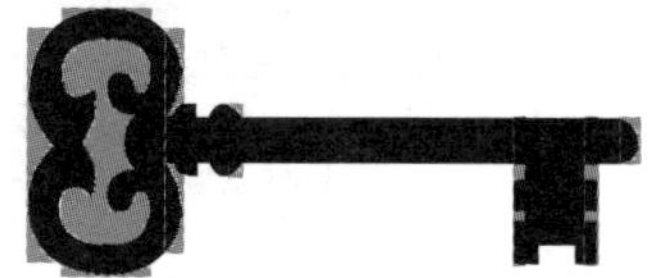

KEY STRATEGIES FOR SUCCESS ON EXAMS

There are many different ways to assess your knowledge and understanding of course concepts. Depending on the subject, your knowledge and skills are most often assessed through a combination of methods which may include performances, demonstrations, projects, products, and oral and written tests. Written exams are one of the most common methods currently used in schools. Just as there are some study strategies that help you to improve your academic performance, there are also some test writing strategies that may help you to do better on unit test and year-end exams. To do your best on any test, you need to be well prepared. You must know the course content and be as familiar as possible with the manner in which it is usually tested. Applying test writing strategies may help you to become more successful on exams, improve your grades, and achieve your potential.

STUDY OPTIONS FOR EXAM PREPARATION

Studying and preparing for exams requires a strong sense of self-discipline. Sometimes having a study buddy or joining a study group

- helps you to stick to your study schedule
- ensures you have others with whom you can practice making and answering sample questions
- clarifies information and provides peer support

It may be helpful to use a combination of individual study, working with a study buddy, or joining a study group to prepare for your unit test or year-end exam. Be sure that the study buddy or group you choose to work with is positive, knowledgeable, motivated, and supportive. Working with a study buddy or a study group usually means you have to begin your exam preparation earlier than you would if you are studying independently.

Tutorial classes are often helpful in preparing for exams. You can ask a knowledgeable student to tutor you or you can hire a private tutor. Sometimes school jurisdictions or individual schools may offer tutorials and study sessions to assist students in preparing for exams. Tutorial services are also offered by companies that specialize in preparing students for exams. Information regarding tutorial services is usually available from school counsellors, local telephone directories, and on-line search engines.

📖 EXAM QUESTION FORMATS

There is no substitute for knowing the course content. To do well in your course you need to combine your subject knowledge and understanding with effective test writing skills. Being familiar with question formats may help you in preparing for quizzes, unit tests or year-end exams. The most typical question formats include multiple choice, numerical response, written response, and essay. The following provides a brief description of each format and suggestions for how you might consider responding to each of the formats.

MULTIPLE CHOICE

A multiple choice question provides some information for you to consider and then requires you to select a response from four choices, often referred to as distracters. The distracters may complete a statement, be a logical extension or application of the information. In preparing for multiple choice questions you may wish to focus on:

- studying concepts, theories, groups of facts or ideas that are similar in meaning; **compare and contrast their similarities and differences**; ask yourself "How do the concepts differ?", "Why is the difference important?", "What does each fact or concept mean or include?" "What are the exceptions?"
- **identifying main ideas, key information**, formulas, concepts, and theories, where they apply and what the **exceptions** are
- memorizing important definitions, examples, and applications of key concepts
- learning to **recognize** *distracters* that may lead you to apply plausible but incorrect solutions, and *three and one splits* where one answer is obviously incorrect and the others are very similar in meaning or wording
- **using active reading techniques** such as underlining, highlighting, numbering, and circling important facts, dates, basic points
- making up your own multiple choice questions for practice

NUMERICAL RESPONSE

A numerical response question provides information and requires you to use a calculation to arrive at the response. In preparing for numerical response questions you may wish to focus on:

- memorizing formulas and their applications
- completing chapter questions or making up your own for practice
- making a habit of **estimating the answer** prior to completing the calculation
- paying special **attention to accuracy** in computing and the use of significant digits where applicable

WRITTEN RESPONSE

A written response question requires you to respond to a question or directive such as "explain", "compare", contrast". In preparing for written response questions you may wish to focus on:

- ensuring your response **answers the question**
- recognizing **directing words** such as "list", "explain", "define"
- providing **concise answers** within the time limit you are devoting to the written response section of the exam
- identifying subject content that lends itself to short answer questions

ESSAY

An essay is a lengthier written response requiring you to identify your position on an issue and provide logical thinking or evidence that supports the basis of your argument. In preparing for an essay you may wish to focus on:

- examining **issues** that are relevant or related to the subject area or **application of the concept**
- comparing and contrasting two points of view, articles, or theories
- considering the merits of the opposite point of view
- identifying **key concepts**, principles or ideas
- providing **evidence**, examples, and **supporting information** for your viewpoint
- preparing two or three essays on probable topics
- **writing an outline** and essay within the defined period of time you will have for the exam
- understanding the "marker's expectations"

📖 *KEY* TIPS FOR ANSWERING COMMON EXAM QUESTION FORMATS

Most exams use a variety of question formats to test your understanding. You must provide responses to questions ranging from lower level, information recall types to higher level, critical thinking types. The following information provides you with some suggestions on how to prepare for answering multiple choice, written response and essay questions.

MULTIPLE CHOICE

Multiple choice questions often require you to make fine distinctions between correct and nearly correct answers so it is imperative that you:

- begin by answering only the questions for which you are certain of the correct answer
- read the question stem and formulate your own response before you read the choices available
- read the directions carefully paying close attention to words such as "mark *all* correct", "choose the *most* correct" and "choose the *one best* answer"
- use active reading techniques such as underlining, circling, or highlighting critical words and phrases
- watch for superlatives such as "all", "every", "none", "always" which indicate that the correct response must be an undisputed fact
- watch for negatives such as "none", "never", "neither", "not" which indicate that the correct response must be an undisputed fact
- examine all of the alternatives in questions which include "all of the above" or "none of the above" as responses to ensure that "all" or "none" of the statements apply *totally*
- be aware of distracters that may lead you to apply plausible but incorrect solutions, and 'three and one splits' where one answer is obviously incorrect and the others are very similar in meaning or wording
- use information from other questions to help you
- eliminate the responses you know are wrong and then assess the remaining alternatives and choose the best one
- guess if you are not certain

WRITTEN RESPONSE

Written response questions usually require a very specific answer. In answering these questions you should:

- underline key words or phrases that indicate what is required in your answer such as "<u>three reasons</u>", "<u>list</u>", or "<u>give an example</u>"
- write down rough, point-form notes regarding the information you want to include in your answer
- be brief and only answer what is asked
- reread your response to ensure you have answered the question
- use the appropriate subject vocabulary and terminology in your response
- use point form to complete as many questions as possible if you are running out of time

ESSAY

Essay questions often give you the opportunity to demonstrate the breadth and depth of your learning regarding a given topic. In responding to these questions it may be helpful to:

- read the question carefully and underline key words and phrases
- make a brief outline to organize the flow of the information and ideas you want to include in your response
- ensure you have an introduction, body, and conclusion
- begin with a clear statement of your view, position, or interpretation of the question
- address only one main point or key idea in each paragraph and include relevant supporting information and examples
- assume the reader has no prior knowledge of your topic
- conclude with a strong summary statement
- use appropriate subject vocabulary and terminology when and where it is applicable
- review your essay for clarity of thought, logic, grammar, punctuation, and spelling
- write as legibly as you can
- double space your work in case you need to edit it when you proof read your essay
- complete the essay in point form if you run short of time

📖 *KEY* TIPS FOR RESPONDING TO COMMON 'DIRECTING' WORDS

There are some commonly used words in exam questions that require you to respond in a predetermined or expected manner.   The following provides you with a brief summary of how you may wish to plan your response to exam questions that contain these words.

- ◆ **EVALUATE** (to assess the worth of something)
    - ▸ Determine the use, goal, or ideal from which you can judge something's worth
    - ▸ Make a value judgment or judgments on something
    - ▸ Make a list of reasons for the judgment
    - ▸ Develop examples, evidence, contrasts, and details to support your judgments and clarify your reasoning

- ◆ **DISCUSS** (usually to give pros and cons regarding an assertion, quotation, or policy)
    - ▸ Make a list of bases for comparing and contrasting
    - ▸ Develop details and examples to support or clarify each pro and con
    - ▸ On the basis of your lists, conclude your response by stating the extent to which you agree or disagree with what is asserted

- ◆ **COMPARE AND CONTRAST** (to give similarities and differences of two or more objects, beliefs, or positions)
    - ▸ Make a list of bases for comparing and contrasting
    - ▸ For each basis, judge similarities and differences
    - ▸ Supply details, evidence, and examples that support and clarify your judgment
    - ▸ Assess the overall similarity or difference
    - ▸ Determine the significance of similarity or difference in connection with the purpose of the comparison

- ◆ **ANALYZE** (to break into parts)
    - ▸ Break the topic, process, procedure, or object of the essay into its major parts
    - ▸ Connect and write about the parts according to the direction of the question: describe, explain, criticize

- ◆ **CRITICIZE** (to judge strong and weak points of something)
    - ▸ Make a list of the strong points and weak points

▸ Develop details, examples, and contrasts to support judgments

▸ Make an overall judgment of quality

♦ **EXPLAIN** (to show causes of or reasons for something)

▸ In Science, usually show the process that occurs in moving from one state or phase in a process to the next, thoroughly presenting details of each step

▸ In Humanities and often in Social Sciences, make a list of factors that influence something, developing evidence for each factor's potential influence

♦ **DESCRIBE** (to give major features of something)

▸ Pick out highlights or major aspects of something

▸ Develop details and illustrations to give a clear picture

♦ **ARGUE** (to give reasons for one position and against another)

▸ Make a list of reasons for the position

▸ Make a list of reasons against the position

▸ Refute objections to your reasons for and defend against objections to your reasons opposing the position

▸ Fill out reasons, objections, and replies with details, examples, consequences, and logical connections

♦ **COMMENT** (to make statements about something)

▸ Calls for a position, discussion, explanation, judgment, or evaluation regarding a subject, idea, or situation

▸ Is strengthened by providing supporting evidence, information, and examples

♦ **DEMONSTRATE** (to show something)

▸ Depending upon the nature of the subject matter, provide evidence, clarify the logical basis of something, appeal to principles or laws as in an explanation, supply a range of opinion and examples

♦ **SYNTHESIZE** (to invent a new or different version)

▸ Construct your own meaning based upon your knowledge and experiences

▸ Support your assertion with examples, references to literature and research studies

(Source: http://www.counc.ivic.ca/learn/program/hndouts/simple.html)

📖 TEST ANXIETY

Do you get test anxiety? Most students feel some level of stress, worry, or anxiety before an exam. Feeling a little tension or anxiety before or during an exam is normal for most students. A little stress or tension may help you rise to the challenge but too much stress or anxiety interferes with your ability to do well on the exam. Test anxiety may cause you to experience some of the following in a mild or more severe form:

- "butterflies" in your stomach, sweating, shortness of breath, or a quickened pulse

- disturbed sleep or eating patterns

- increased nervousness, fear, or irritability

- sense of hopelessness or panic

- drawing a "blank" during the exam

If you experience extreme forms of test anxiety you need to consult your family physician. For milder forms of anxiety you may find some of the following strategies effective in helping you to remain calm and focused during your unit tests or year-end exams.

- Acknowledge that you are feeling some stress or test anxiety and that this is normal

- Focus upon your breathing, taking several deep breaths

- Concentrate upon a single object for a few moments

- Tense and relax the muscles in areas of your body where you feel tension

- Break your exam into smaller, manageable, achievable parts

- Use positive self-talk to calm and motivate yourself. Tell yourself, "I can do this if I read carefully/start with the easy questions/focus on what I know/stick with it/. . ." instead of saying, "I can't do this."

- Visualize your successful completion of your review or the exam

- Recall a time in the past when you felt calm, relaxed, and content. Replay this experience in your mind experiencing it as fully as possible.

KEY STRATEGIES FOR SUCCESS BEFORE AN EXAM – A CHECKLIST

Review, review, review. That's a huge part of your exam preparation. Here's a quick review checklist for you to see how many strategies for success you are using as you prepare to write your unit tests and year-end exams.

KEY Strategies for Success Before an Exam	*Yes*	*No*
Have you been attending classes?		
Have you determined your learning style?		
Have you organized a quiet study area for yourself?		
Have you developed a long-term study schedule?		
Have you developed a short-term study schedule?		
Are you working with a study buddy or study group?		
Is your study buddy/group positive, knowledgeable, motivated and supportive?		
Have you registered in tutorial classes?		
Have you developed your exam study notes?		
Have you reviewed previously administered exams?		
Have you practiced answering multiple choice, numerical response, written response, and essay questions?		
Have you analyzed the most common errors students make on each subject exam?		
Have you practiced strategies for controlling your exam anxiety?		
Have you maintained a healthy diet and sleep routine?		
Have you participated in regular physical activity?		

📖 *KEY* STRATEGIES FOR SUCCESS DURING AN EXAM

Doing well on any exam requires that you prepare in advance by reviewing your subject material and then using your knowledge to respond effectively to the exam questions during the test session. Combining subject knowledge with effective test writing skills gives you the best opportunity for success. The following are some strategies you may find useful in writing your exam.

- ◆ Managing Test Anxiety
  - ‣ Be as prepared as possible to increase your self-confidence.
  - ‣ Arrive at the exam on time and bring whatever materials you need to complete the exam such as pens, pencils, erasers, and calculators if they are allowed.
  - ‣ Drink enough water before you begin the exam so you are hydrated.
  - ‣ Associate with positive, calm individuals until you enter the exam room.
  - ‣ Use positive self-talk to calm yourself.
  - ‣ Remind yourself that it is normal to feel anxious about the exam.
  - ‣ Visualize your successful completion of the exam.
  - ‣ Breathe deeply several times.
  - ‣ Rotate your head, shrug your shoulders, and change positions to relax.

- ◆ While the information from your crib notes is still fresh in your memory, write down the key words, concepts, definitions, theories or formulas on the back of the test paper before you look at the exam questions.
  - ‣ Review the entire exam.
  - ‣ Budget your time.
  - ‣ Begin with the easiest question or the question that you know you can answer correctly rather than following the numerical question order of the exam.
  - ‣ Be aware of linked questions and use the clues to help you with other questions or in other parts of the exam.

If you "blank" on the exam, try repeating the deep breathing and physical relaxation activities first. Then move to visualization and positive self-talk to get you going. You can also try to open the 'information flow' by writing down anything that you remember about the subject on the reverse side of your exam paper. This activity sometimes helps you to remind yourself that you <u>do</u> know something and you are capable of writing the exam.

📖 GETTING STARTED

MANAGING YOUR TIME

- Plan on staying in the exam room for the full time that is available to you.

- Review the entire exam and calculate how much time you can spend on each section. Write your time schedule on the top of your paper and stick as closely as possible to the time you have allotted for each section of the exam.

- Be strategic and use your time where you will get the most marks. Avoid spending too much time on challenging questions that are not worth more marks than other questions that may be easier and are worth the same number of marks.

- If you are running short of time, switch to point form and write as much as you can for written response and essay questions so you have a chance of receiving partial marks.

- Leave time to review your paper asking yourself, "Did I do all of the questions I was supposed to do?", "Can I answer any questions now that I skipped over before?", "Are there any questions that I misinterpreted or misread?"

USING THE FIVE PASS METHOD

- **BROWSING STAGE** – Scan the entire exam noting the format, the specific instructions and marks allotted for each section, which questions you will complete and which ones you will omit if there is a choice.

- **THE FIRST ANSWERING PASS** – To gain confidence and momentum, answer only the questions you are confident you can answer correctly and quickly. These questions are most often found in the multiple choice or numerical response sections of the exam. Maintain a brisk pace; if a question is taking too long to answer, leave it for the Second or Third Pass.

- **THE SECOND ANSWERING PASS** – This Pass addresses questions which require more effort per mark. Answer as many of the remaining questions as possible while maintaining steady progress toward a solution. As soon as it becomes evident the question is too difficult or is tasking an inordinate amount of time, leave it for the Third Answering Pass.

- **THE THIRD ANSWERING PASS** – During the Third Answering Pass you should complete all partial solutions from the first two Passes. Marks are produced at a slower rate during this stage. At the end of this stage, all questions should have full or partial answers. Guess at any multiple choice questions that you have not yet answered.

- **THE FINAL REVIEW STAGE** – Use the remaining time to review the entire exam, making sure that no questions have been overlooked. Check answers and calculations as time permits.

USING THE THREE PASS METHOD

- **OVERVIEW** – Begin with an overview of the exam to see what it contains. Look for 'easy' questions and questions on topics that you know thoroughly.

- **SECOND PASS** – Answer all the questions that you can complete without too much trouble. These questions help to build your confidence and establish a positive start.

- **LAST PASS** – Now go through and answer the questions that are left. This is when you begin to try solving the questions you find particularly challenging.

📖 *KEY* EXAM TIPS FOR SELECTED SUBJECT AREAS

The following are a few additional suggestions you may wish to consider when writing exams in any of the selected subject areas.

ENGLISH LANGUAGE ARTS

Exams in English Language Arts usually have two components, writing and reading. Sometimes students are allowed to bring approved reference books such as a dictionary, thesaurus and writing handbook into the exam. If you have not used these references on a regular basis, you may find them more of a hindrance than a help in an exam situation. In completing the written section of an English Language Arts exam:

- plan your essay

- focus on the issue presented

- establish a clear position using a thesis statement to direct and unify your writing

- organize your writing in a manner that logically presents your views

- support your viewpoint with specific examples

- edit and proof read your writing

In completing the reading section of an English Language Arts exam:

- read the entire selection before responding

- use titles, dates, footnotes, pictures, introductions, and notes on the author to assist you in developing an understanding of the piece presented

- when using line references, read a few lines before and after the identified section

MATHEMATICS

In some instances, the use of calculators is permitted (or required) to complete complex calculations, modeling, simulations, or to demonstrate your use of technology. It is imperative that you are familiar with the approved calculator and the modes you may be using during your exam. In writing exams in mathematics:

- use appropriate mathematical notation and symbols
- clearly show or explain all the steps involved in solving the problem
- check to bc sure you have included the correct units of measurement and have rounded to the appropriate significant digit
- use appropriate labelling and equal increments on graphs

SCIENCES

In the Sciences written response and open-ended questions usually require a clear, organized, and detailed explanation of the science involved in the question. You may find it helpful to use the acronym **STEEPLES** to organize your response to these types of questions. STEEPLES stands for **S**cience, **T**echnological, **E**cological, **E**thical, **P**olitical, **L**egal, **E**conomical, and **S**ocial aspects of the issue presented. In writing exams in the sciences:

- use scientific vocabulary to clearly explain your understanding of the processes or issues
- state your position in an objective manner
- demonstrate your understanding of both sides of the issue
- clearly label graphs, diagrams, tables, and charts using accepted conventions
- provide all formulas and equations

SOCIAL STUDIES, HISTORY, GEOGRAPHY

Exams in these courses of study often require you to take a position on an issue and defend your point of view. Your response should demonstrate your understanding of both the positive and negative aspects of the issue and be supported by well-considered arguments and evidence. In writing exams in Social Studies, History or Geography, the following acronyms may be helpful to you in organizing your approach.

- **SEE** – stands for **S**tatement, **E**xplanation, **E**xample. This acronym reminds you to couple your statement regarding your position with an explanation and then an example.

- **PERMS** – stands for **P**olitical, **E**conomic, **R**eligious or moral, **M**ilitary, and **S**ocietal values. Your position statement may be derived from or based upon any of these points of view. Your argument is more credible if you can show that recognized authorities such as leaders, theorists, writers or scientists back your position.

📖 SUMMARY

Writing exams involves a certain amount of stress and anxiety. If you want to do your best on the exam, *there is no substitute for being well prepared.* Being well prepared helps you to feel more confident about your ability to succeed and less anxious about writing tests. In preparing for unit or year-end exams remember to:

- use as many senses as possible in preparing for exams
- start as early as possible set realistic goals and targets
- take advantage of study buddies, study groups, and tutorials
- review previously used exams
- study with positive, knowledgeable, motivated, and supportive individuals
- practice the material in the format in which you are to be tested
- try to simulate the test situation as much as possible
- keep a positive attitude
- end your study time with a quick review and then do something different before you try to go to sleep on the night before the exam
- drink a sufficient amount of water prior to an exam
- stay in the exam room for the full amount of time available
- try to relax by focusing on your breathing

If you combine your best study habits with some of the strategies presented here, you may increase your chances of writing a strong exam and maximizing your potential to do well.

NOTES

PRACTICE EXAMINATIONS

A GUIDE TO PREPARING FOR AN EXAMINATION

The questions presented here are distinct from those in the Unit Review section.
THE KEY contains detailed answers that illustrate the problem-solving process for every question in this section.

Students are encouraged to write these practice exams under conditions similar to those they will encounter when writing their final exam. This will make students:

- *aware of the mental and physical stamina required to sit through an entire exam*
- *familiar with the exam format and how the course content is tested*
- *aware of any units or concepts that are troublesome or require additional study*
- *more successful in managing their review effectively*

To simulate the exam conditions students should:

- *use an alarm clock or other timer to monitor the time allowed for the exams*
- *select a quiet writing spot away from all distractions*
- *assemble the appropriate materials that are allowed for writing the exams such as pens, HB pencils, calculator, dictionary*
- *use "test wiseness" skills*
- *complete as much of the exams as possible within the allowable time*

In writing the practice exams students should:

- *read instructions, directions and questions carefully*
- *organize writing time according to the exam emphasis on each section*
- *highlight key words*
- *think about what is being asked*
- *plan their writing; once complete, proof for errors in content, spelling, grammar*
- *watch for bolded words such as most, least, best*
- *in Multiple Choice questions, cross out any choices students know are incorrect*
- *if possible, review all responses upon completion of the exams*

PRACTICE EXAMINATIONS

Suggested writing time for each Practice Examination: 45 minutes

The practice examinations each contain four or five passages. Each passage is followed by multiple-choice questions that test your knowledge and comprehension. Some questions may require you to make connections between two passages.

Some passages are preceded by short context statement that may help you to better understand the passage. Some passages contain footnotes that may aid your comprehension.

The numbers in the left margin next to passages are for reference purposes. Every fifth paragraph is numbered 5, 10, 15, and so on. For poetry, every fifth line is numbered 5, 10, 15, and so on.

Read each context statement, passage, footnote and question carefully, then decide the best answer for each question and mark the correct answer.

Take the smart route to university

6 Bachelor's Degrees
26 Career Programs
Over 500 university courses
Plus 10 ways to upgrade

Planning to complete a degree?

You can finish a Bachelor's degree at Douglas College, or complete your first two years here and go straight into third year at university. Students choose Douglas College because we provide excellent professors, smaller classes, competitive fees (save $3,000 or more) and two handy Lower Mainland campus locations.

For more information about all our university transfer and career programs, visit our web site, call 604-527-5478 or email registrar_office@douglas.bc.ca

Douglas College

New Westminster Campus
700 Royal Avenue (one block from the New Westminster SkyTrain Station)

David Lam Campus
1250 Pinetree Way, Coquitlam (one km north of Coquitlam Centre Mall)

douglascollege.ca

You can go anywhere from here

Get where you want to go… fast!

- √ high job placement rates
- √ unmatched selection of practical programs in a range of fields
- √ flexibility — full- or part-time; classroom or distance education; certificates, diplomas and degrees
- √ academic learning combined with real-world, hands-on training
- √ approachable, industry-experienced instructors

www.bcit.ca

The path you choose can make all the difference.

BUSINESS & MEDIA, COMPUTING & INFORMATION TECHNOLOGY, **ENGINEERING, APPLIED & NATURAL SCIENCES,** HEALTH SCIENCES, **TRADES**

Camosun College in Victoria ...for the best in Learning and Lifestyle

Applied Chemistry & Biotechnology
Applied Communication
Apprenticeship Training
Associate of Arts Degree
Associate of Science Degree
Automotive Mechanical Repair
Bachelor of Business Administration –
 Accounting Major
Better Employment Strategies & Techniques
Business Administration
Carpentry
Certified Dental Assistant
Civil Engineering Technology
Community, Family & Child Studies
Community Mental Health Worker
Community Support Worker
Computer Graphics Technician, Engineering
Computer Systems Technology
Criminal Justice
Culinary Arts
Dental Hygiene
Early Childhood Care & Education
Electrical
Electronics & Computer Engineering
 Technology
English as a Second Language
Environmental Technology
Exercise & Wellness
Fine Furniture
First Nations Community Studies
First Nations Family Support Worker
First Nations Home Support /
 Resident Care Attendant
Golf Management
Heavy Duty / Commercial Transport Mechanics
Home Support / Resident Care Attendant
Horticulture Technician
Hospital Unit Clerk
Hotel & Restaurant Management
Human Resource Management
Legal Office Assistant
Manufacturing Technician
Mechanical Engineering Technology
Medical Laboratory Assistant
Medical Office Assistant
Music
Nautical Training
Network & Electronics Technician
Nursing
Office Administration
Plumbing & Pipe Trades
Pharmacy Technician
Practical Nursing
Public Administration
Sheet Metal Technician
Tourism
Travel Counselling
University Transfer Arts, Science & Business
Visual Arts
Welding

Learning at Camosun:

- The ideal mix of in-class academics and hands-on practical experience.

- Small class sizes, lower tuition, dedicated faculty.

- Transfer credit to university degree programs throughout BC and beyond.

- Extra services to help you succeed, like language and math labs, academic advising, learning skills seminars, and the student employment centre.

- Welcoming close to 8,000 students each year including more than 700 International students from around the world.

Living on Southern Vancouver Island:

- Greater Victoria is friendly, safe, clean and easy to get around on foot, bicycle or bus.

- The moderate climate is ideal for year-round outdoor activities such as cycling, hiking, sailing, golfing, fishing, kayaking and more!

- You'll find lots to do on the weekends, including many cultural celebrations, historical and scenic landmarks, and great shopping!

CAMOSUN COLLEGE

Start your degree.
Start your career. Start *here!*

Win a 4GB iPod nano! Log onto camosun.ca/nano to find out how.

LANGARA COLLEGE
Business & Management ■ Creative & Applied Arts ■ Health & Human Services ■ Liberal Arts & Languages ■ Science & Technology ■ Social & Cultural Studies

Langara College has earned a reputation for academic excellence in providing Arts & Science University Transfer, Career, and Continuing Studies Programs.

More students transfer to BC universities from Langara College than from any other college in the province, and more than 90 percent of our career program grads find employment in their chosen field within four months of graduation.

In an increasingly complex world, knowledge is freedom.

Learn more.

Langara College | 100 West 49 Avenue, Vancouver, BC | Canada | V5Y 2Z6 | 604.323.5686 | www.langara.bc.ca

Trinity Western University

UNDERGRADUATE:

Applied Mathematics with Computer Science

Art

Biblical Studies

Biology

Biotechnology

Business Administration

Chemistry

Christianity and Culture

Communications

Computing Science

Drama

Education

English

Environmental Studies

European Studies

Fine Arts

General Studies

Geography

History

Humanities

Human Kinetics

Human Services

Inter-Cultural Religious Studies

International Studies

Linguistics

Mathematics

Modern Languages

Music

Natural and Applied Sciences

Nursing

Philosophy

Political Studies

Pre-Professional Studies
• Pre-Dentistry • Pre-Med •
Pre-Pharmacy • Pre-Vet

Psychology

Religious Studies

Social Sciences

Sport & Leisure Management

Serving up options

from Canada's premier Christian university

INGREDIENTS: a special blend of quality programs, outstanding faculty, firm faith foundation, groundbreaking research, dynamic student life, whole person development, and $2 million in scholarships.

APPLY TODAY   1.888.GO.TO.TWU   www.twu.ca/undergraduate

The CKNW Orphans' Fund is dedicated to promoting the health and welfare of disadvantaged children. It assists by allocating funds generously donated by dedicated CKNW listeners, local businesses, and through sound investments and thoughtful bequests.

The CKNW Orphan's Fund has a long history of compassion and assistance to disadvantaged children in the Lower Mainland. Through the Partners in Education program sponsored by Castle Rock Research, B.C., the Orphan's Fund has made a generous contribution of The Key Study Guides to these children.

For more information on the Orphans' Fund please go to

www.cknw.com

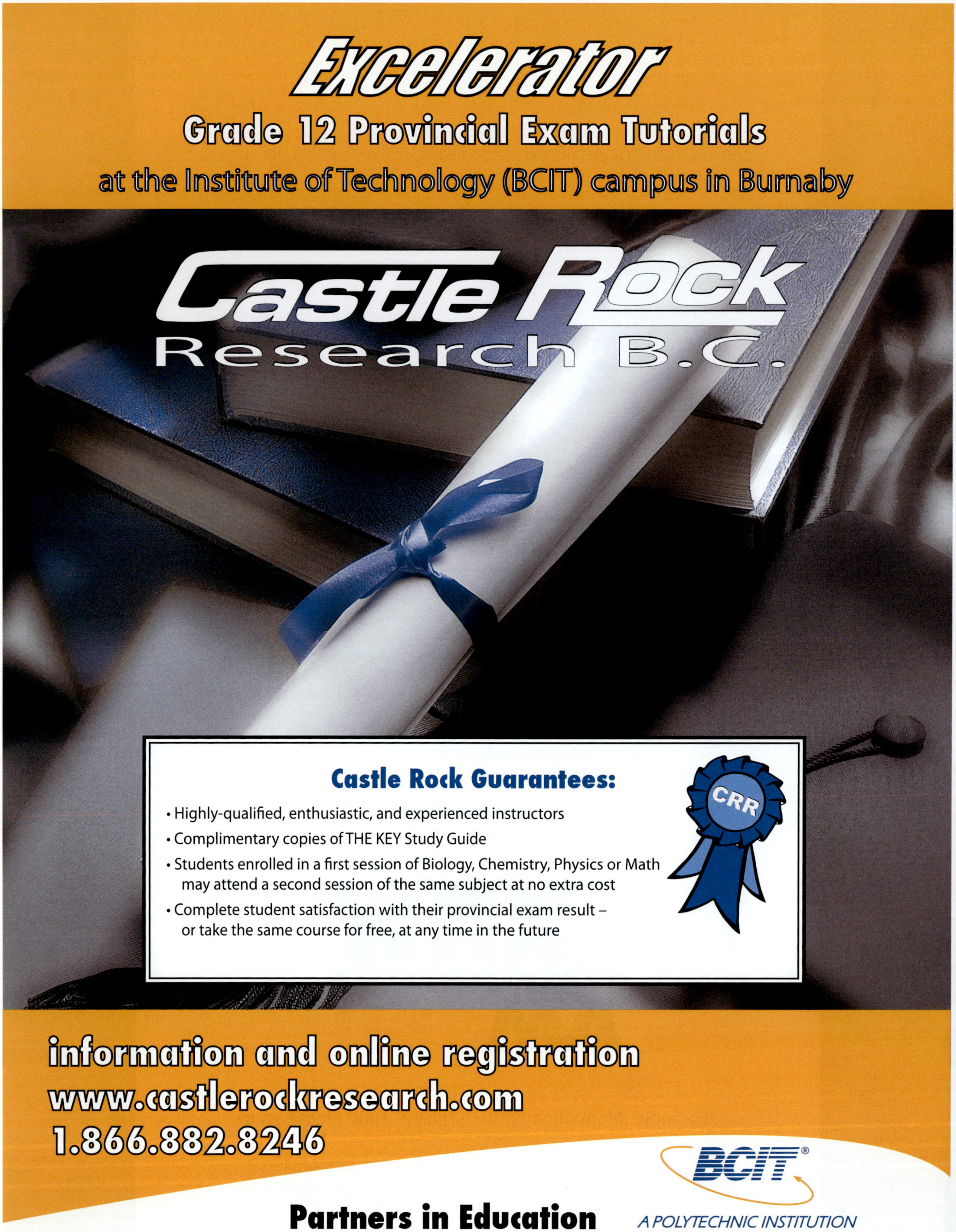

Excelerator
Grade 12 Provincial Exam Tutorials
at the Institute of Technology (BCIT) campus in Burnaby

Castle Rock
Research B.C.

Castle Rock Guarantees:

- Highly-qualified, enthusiastic, and experienced instructors
- Complimentary copies of THE KEY Study Guide
- Students enrolled in a first session of Biology, Chemistry, Physics or Math may attend a second session of the same subject at no extra cost
- Complete student satisfaction with their provincial exam result – or take the same course for free, at any time in the future

information and online registration
www.castlerockresearch.com
1.866.882.8246

Partners in Education

A POLYTECHNIC INSTITUTION

PRACTICE EXAMINATION 1

Reading One

From *Emma*

Emma Woodhouse, handsome, clever, and rich, with a comfortable home and happy disposition, seemed to unite some of the best blessings of existence; and had lived nearly twenty-one years in the world with very little to distress or vex her.

She was the youngest of the two daughters of a most affectionate, indulgent father; and had, in consequence of her sister Isabella's marriage, been mistress of his house from a very early period. Her mother had died too long ago for her to have more than an indistinct remembrance of her caresses; and her place had been supplied by an excellent woman as governess, who had fallen little short of a mother in affection.

Sixteen years had Miss Taylor been in Mr. Woodhouse's family, less as a governess than a friend, very fond of both daughters, but particularly of Emma. Between them it was more the intimacy of sisters. Even before Miss Taylor had ceased to hold the nominal office of governess, the mildness of her temper had hardly allowed her to impose any restraint; and the shadow of authority being now long passed away, they had been living together as friend and friend very mutually attached, and Emma doing just what she liked; highly esteeming Miss Taylor's judgment, but directed chiefly by her own.

The real evils, indeed, of Emma's situation were the power of having rather too much her own way, and a disposition to think a little too well of herself; these were the disadvantages which threatened alloy to her many enjoyments. The danger, however, was at present so unperceived, that they did not by any means rank as misfortunes with her.

5   Sorrow came—a gentle sorrow—but not at all in the shape of any disagreeable consciousness. Miss Taylor married. It was Miss Taylor's loss which first brought grief. It was on the wedding-day of this beloved friend that Emma first sat in mournful thought of any continuance. The wedding over, and the   bride-people gone, her father and herself were left to dine together, with no prospect of a third to cheer a long evening. Her father composed himself to sleep after dinner, as usual, and she had then only to sit and think of what she had lost.

The event had every promise of happiness for her friend. Mr. Weston was a man of unexceptionable character, easy fortune, suitable age, and pleasant manners; and there was some satisfaction in considering with what self-denying, generous friendship she had always wished and promoted the match; but it was a black morning's work for her. The want of Miss Taylor would be felt every hour of every day. She recalled her past kindness—the kindness, the affection of sixteen years—how she had taught and how she had played with her from five years old—how she had devoted all her powers to attach and amuse her in health—and how she nursed her through the various illnesses of childhood. A large debt of gratitude was owing here; but the intercourse of the last seven years, the equal footing and perfect unreserve which had soon followed Isabella's marriage, on their being left to each other, was yet a dearer, tenderer recollection. She had been a friend and companion such as few possessed: intelligent, well-informed, useful, gentle, knowing all the ways of the family, interested in all its concerns, and peculiarly interested in herself, in every pleasure, every scheme of hers—one to whom she could speak every thought as it arose, and who had such an affection for her as could never find fault.

How was she to bear the change?—It was true that her friend was going only half a mile from them; but Emma was aware that great must be the difference between a Mrs. Weston, only half a mile from them, and a Miss Taylor in the house; and with all her advantages, natural and domestic, she was now in great danger of suffering from intellectual solitude. She dearly loved her father, but he was no companion for her. He could not meet her in conversation, rational or playful.

The evil of the actual disparity in their ages (and Mr. Woodhouse had not married early) was much increased by his constitution and habits; for having been a valetudinarian[1] all his life, without activity of mind or body, he was a much older man in ways than in years; and though everywhere beloved for the friendliness of his heart and his amiable temper, his talents could not have recommended him at any time.

Jane Austen

1. Which of the following statements gives the **main** theme of the passage?

    A. Best friends often desert each other.

    B. Employees might become family members.

    C. Parents do not always relate well to their children.

    D. It is sometimes difficult to accept life's changes.

2. According to this passage, the "real evils" (paragraph 4) of Emma's situation are related to the fact that

    A. she lives in the countryside.

    B. her mother passed away at an early age.

    C. she has no brothers to protect her.

    D. she has gotten used to getting her own way.

3. About how old is Emma when Miss Taylor gets married?

    A. 5 years of age

    B. 7 years of age

    C. 16 years of age

    D. 21 years of age

---

[1] valetudinarian—someone who is weak or sickly

4. From the context of the passage, what does the word "nominal" (paragraph 3) most probably mean?

    A. In name only

    B. To nominate

    C. Costly

    D. Insignificant

5. What is "the change" (paragraph 7) that Emma finds nearly unbearable?

    A. Her sister is gone.

    B. She cannot visit her friend now that she has gotten married.

    C. The governess has married.

    D. Her father has decided to remarry the governess.

6. Which of the following phrases **best** describes Mr. Weston's character?

    A. He was easy-going and well-to-do.

    B. He was irritable and high-strung.

    C. He was relaxed and basically lazy.

    D. He lived half a mile away.

7. The relationship between Emma and Miss Taylor is **best** described as

    A. close

    B. sisterly

    C. deteriorating

    D. self-serving

Reading Two

Imagine the night sky as you read this poem.

Stars

Now in the West the slender moon lies low,
And now Orion[1] glimmers through the trees,
Clearing the earth with even pace and slow,
And now the stately-moving Pleiades,[2]
5   In that soft infinite darkness overhead
Hang jewel-wise upon a silver thread.

And all the lonelier stars that have their place,
Calm lamps within the distant southern sky,
And planet-dust upon the edge of space,
10   Look down upon the fretful world, and I
Look up to outer vastness unafraid
And see the stars which sang when earth was made.

Marjorie Pickthall

8. Which of the following statements gives the **main** idea of the poem?

A. Nature has a powerful effect on humans.

B. The moon and the stars light up the sky at night.

C. Constellations are named after humans.

D. The moon calms our fears.

9. What is the rhyme scheme of the poem?

A. abab

B. abba

C. abcabc

D. ababcc

---

[1] *Orion*—a constellation taking the form of a hunter with a belt and a sword.

[2] *Pleiades*— in Greek myth, the seven daughters of Atlas, and a group of stars in the constellation Taurus, not far from Orion.

10. The purpose of the personification of Orion and Pleiades is to illustrate

    A. how much these constellations are like people

    B. how slowly they moved

    C. the beauty of the lights shining out of the dark sky

    D. the grace and majesty of the constellations as they move across the sky

11. What does the description of the slender moon as lying low (line 1) indicate about the moon?

    A. It was not in a vertical position.

    B. It was full.

    C. It was about to set in the west.

    D. It was waning rather than waxing.

12. Which of the five senses is **most strongly** evoked in this poem?

    A. Smell

    B. Touch

    C. Taste

    D. Sight

Reading Three

What amazing things can technology do?

Closet of the future picks out clothes

TOKYO—Japan's leading electronics companies are hard at work trying to make the country's notoriously cramped houses smarter—and more convenient—with a high-tech touch.

At its new Tokyo showroom, Matsushita Electric Industrial Co., maker of the Panasonic brand, is enticing Japan's gadget lovers with two model "houses of tomorrow."

On show are a toilet that analyzes your urine and automatically sends suspicious results to the doctor via the Internet, and a closet that picks out clothes according to weather forecasts—and whether you need to impress the boss.

Not sure what to wear for that high school reunion? Just ask your closet. Wondering how to get rid of that pimple on your chin? Consult the mirror for advice on clear skin.

5 "These are ideas that in a few years we'll be able in some way to sell." Matsushita spokesman Wilson Solano said. "This is market potential."

The products went on display last week. They aren't even priced yet, and are slated to go to market in 2005 or beyond.

Meagre Japanese abodes are infamous for paper-thin walls and tight quarters. Floor space averages only 32.5 square metres, which is barely half a storey in a typical North American house.

But the trend is clear. What they lack in size, some are trying to make up in smarts. Toilets flush by remote control and have motorized seats that adjust to your height. Lights are primed to switch on when someone walks in a room. And the Japanese have been adopting high-speed Internet access much faster than Americans.

Part of Matsushita's push are products that afford extra elbow room.

10 That includes the all-in-one washer-dryer, especially useful in Japan where the typical washing machine is only half as big as its American counterpart and where most people hang clothes outside.

Matsushita also introduced a kitchen table with a touch-screen computer built into it that doubles as a flat-screen television.

It's not the only company trying to tap cravings for creature comforts.

Sharp Corp. presently unveiled an air conditioner that supposedly kills the flu bug, while Sanyo Electric Co. has a bed sheet that monitors a sleeper's breathing, heart rates and body movement to adjust the room's heat and lighting for a good night's rest.

Back at Matsushita's showroom, some gadgets actually take up more space than their forerunners. There's the oversized refrigerator with a built-in camera that beams pictures to your mobile phone so you can check if you're low on milk while cruising the dairy aisle.

15   The company also offers an electromagnetic stove and countertop. Its heating elements won't burn fingers on touch but will warm up pans when covered, while the counter automatically powers a special line of cordless kitchen appliances.

There is also the "laboratory toilet" that tests your urine to measure blood sugar, protein and body fat.

Not to be outdone is the automated closet. Users simply punch in today's weather and preferred clothing style—such as casual or formal—and let the computer sort out the rest. Between wearings, the wardrobe also treats your garments to a steam cleaning.

And for those in need of a live-in beautician, there's the Matsushita bathroom sink ensemble. Its mirror takes infrared pictures of your hair and skin, keeps the record in its data banks and recommends the treatment to bring out that shine. It also dispenses mineral waters in varying degrees of acidity to best suit your ailment.

The developments are similar to luxuries being dabbled with in the United States but mostly reserved for the privileged few.

20   Microsoft mogul Bill Gates' multi-million mansion outside Seattle features a computer system that changes music, temperature, lighting and even digital artwork to match visitor preferences as people move from room to room.

Japanese consumers are similarly renowned for being gizmo-crazy, and line up for the latest in everything from mobile phones to digital cameras.

That's just the kind of customer Matsushita is banking on.

"The strength of this company is they know what the consumers want," Solano said. "They want to have it simple, where you can just press a button."

Hans Greimel

13.   The **main** purpose of this article is to

    A. persuade readers to buy more electronics

    B. describe new and unusual hi-tech products

    C. explain what life is like in Japan

    D. market luxurious products to the masses

14.   What is the companies' main purpose in displaying these products?

    A. To inform the public about their products

    B. To stimulate sales of their products

    C. To advertise their products

    D. To educate the public about their products

15. According to the article, a reason that Japanese companies are trying to develop these high-tech products is to

   A. win international awards in innovation

   B. make cramped houses more comfortable

   C. make the country more efficient

   D. allow houses to be larger and warmer

16. Why would an all-in-one washer-dryer be beneficial?

   A. It could be placed outside.

   B. It could hold twice as must as an American model.

   C. Most people in Japan don't have washers.

   D. Most people in Japan don't have dryers.

17. How would the new toilet described in paragraphs 3, 8, and 16 benefit the consumer?

   A. It would take up less space in the bathroom.

   B. It would advise the user of skin ailments.

   C. It would detect health problems.

   D. It would switch on when the bathroom is entered.

18. Which of the leading-edge products described in the article use photos as part of the technology?

   A. The refrigerator and the mirror

   B. The refrigerator and the closet

   C. The table and the television

   D. The washer and the digital camera

19. The computer system in Bill Gates' mansion is designed to change the artwork

   A. to adjust to different people's tastes

   B. when it gets tired of the same pictures

   C. when visitors press the buttons on the walls

   D. because different artwork requires different lighting

Reading Four

Table 4:

Percentage of Internet users, aged 15 and over, by selected types of Internet activity, Canada and province, 2000[1]

	Total users	E-mail	E-banking	Purchased goods or services	Information about goods and services	Health information	Chat service	News-groups or listserv	News sites
	(000's)				%				
Canada	12,981	83.6	22.7	23.7	74.3	45.9	30.0	15.7	54.7
Newfoundland	192	81.3	17.4	19.6	73.5	56.8	35.7	16.4	52.9
Prince Edward Island	53	82.3	16.9	18.2	71.5	55.5	28.1	16.9	46.5
Nova Scotia	396	85.9	23.6	23.4	74.8	54.0	33.8	19.2	55.0
New Brunswick	272	78.8	16.6	19.3	72.2	49.2	33.3	14.6	53.5
Quebec	2,723	78.2	21.9	19.3	73.9	40.4	34.0	11.6	55.7
Ontario	5,103	84.5	23.6	25.6	73.1	46.7	29.2	16.8	56.9
Manitoba	412	78.7	16.6	19.8	71.2	46.6	30.2	12.8	51.5
Saskatchewan	396	81.1	16.3	20.3	73.4	45.2	26.2	13.5	44.8
Alberta	1,418	86.9	23.4	25.9	78.2	43.6	30.5	16.1	53.0
British Columbia	2,016	87.8	25.1	26.2	76.2	49.2	25.1	18.5	51.9

[1] Percentage that has ever used the Internet for these activities, except e-mail, which has been used in the past 12 months.
Note: Totals exclude "Not stated."
Source: Statistics Canada, General Social Survey, Cycle 14

20. The format in which the information above is presented is known as a

   A. line graph

   B. bar graph

   C. table

   D. pie chart

21. What is the purpose of this information?

   A. To show how the Internet is used

   B. To show areas in which the Internet could be improved

   C. To convince more people to use the Internet

   D. To promote uses of the Internet

22. According to this information, what was the most popular use of the Internet in Canada in 2000?

   A. To access e-mail

   B. To purchase goods or services

   C. To get information about goods and services

   D. To view news sites

23. In which of the following provinces do Internet users bank on-line the least?

    A. Prince Edward Island

    B. British Columbia

    C. Alberta

    D. Saskatchewan

24. In which of the following provinces do Internet users do the most on-line shopping?

    A. British Columbia

    B. Prince Edward Island

    C. Ontario

    D. Quebec

25. How many Internet users does Quebec have?

    A. 2 723

    B. 782 000

    C. 272 000

    D. 2 723 000

Reading Five

Pantoum[1] for a Mother in Nunavut

The landscape is stark and colorless,
small-town gossip follows you everywhere.
Even in the dingy hotel room, you can't be alone.
The natives hunt fox and their voices carry for miles.

5   Small-town gossip follows you everywhere.
What they say is foreign, is different.
The natives hunt fox and their voices carry for miles.
They covet your expensive laptop, your briefcase.

What they say is foreign, is different:
10   your smile, your naïve thin gloves,
They covet your expensive laptop, your briefcase.
And the telephone is your only escape.

The way you smile, your naïve thin gloves,
lonely in the white of snow.
15   The telephone is your only escape,
on the other end of the line there is warmth.

Lonely in the white of snow,
your hair still smells of west-coast weather.
On the other end of the line there is warmth
20   soft, like cherry blossoms in Victoria's spring.

Your hair still smells of west-coast weather
embroidered wolves on parkas,
soft, like cherry blossoms in Victoria's spring.
You are trapped in a sea of fur-lined hoods.

25   Embroidered wolves on your parka
Don't make you any warmer.
Trapped in a sea of fur-lined hoods,
dreaming of cotton and silk.

Claire Battershill
First Place National Winner
Senior Category
in *Reverse, a Zine for*
Youngpoets

---

[1] *pantoum*—a poetic form in which the second and fourth lines of each four-line stanza become the first and third lines of the next stanza.

26. This poem is **mainly** about

    A. the cold weather in Nunavut

    B. a person away from home

    C. a child phoning her mother

    D. hunters in a small town

27. What does the speaker mean when she says that she "can't be alone"(line 3)?

    A. She has too many meetings to attend.

    B. There are foxes all around.

    C. Even when she is by herself, she knows what people are saying about her.

    D. Even when she is by herself, she becomes very anxious.

28. The detail "naïve thin gloves" (lines 10 and 13) reveals that the mother

    A. left her fancy gloves at home

    B. did not know much about her work

    C. had expensive taste

    D. was unprepared for the cold

29. The main reason that the mother is lonely is that she

    A. feels out of place

    B. can see no cherry blossoms

    C. has to work on her laptop

    D. must phone home every day

30. The phrase "Your hair still smells of west-coast weather" (line 18) is an example of the poetic device of

    A. imagery

    B. paradox

    C. personification

    D. oxymoron

31. Which of the following phrases reveals that the mother wishes she were elsewhere?

    A. "The natives hunt fox"

    B. "Your hair still smells of west-coast weather"

    C. "Embroidered wolves on your parka"

    D. "Dreaming of cotton and silk"

32. How does the mother escape from her situation?

    A. She packs her briefcase.

    B. She phones people she knows.

    C. She goes fox hunting.

    D. She returns to Victoria.

33. Which of the following words **best** describes the feeling that the mother is experiencing?

    A. Alienated

    B. Impatient

    C. Overburdened

    D. Anxious

34. The phrase "there is warmth / soft, like cherry blossoms"(lines 19 to 20) contains an example of

    A. simile

    B. metaphor

    C. oxymoron

    D. hyperbole

35. Which of the following words **best** describes the tone of the poem?

    A. Serious

    B. Gentle

    C. Forgiving

    D. Sarcastic

PRACTICE EXAMINATION 2

Reading One

What should modern poets be writing about?

On the Future of Poetry

Bards[1] of the Future! you that come
With striding march, and roll of drum,
What will your newest challenge be
To our prose-bound community?

5   What magic will you find to stir
The limp and languid listener?
Will it be daring and dramatic?
Will it be frankly democratic?

Will Pegasus[2] return again
10   In guise of modern aeroplane,
Descending from a cloudless blue
To drop on us a bomb or two?

I know not. Far be it from me
To darken dark futurity;
15   Still less to render more perplexed
The last vagary,[3] or the next.

I hold it for a certain thing,
That, blank or rhyming, song must sing;
And more, that what is good for verse,
20   Need not, by dint of rhyme, grow worse.

I hold that they who deal in rhyme
Must take the standpoint of the time—
But not to catch the public ear,
As mountebank[4] or pulpiteer;[5]

25   That the old notes are still the new,
If the musician's touch be true—
Nor can the hand that knows its trade
Achieve the trite and ready-made;

That your first theme is Human Life,
30   Its hopes and fears, its love and strife—
A theme no custom can efface,
Common, but never commonplace.

Henry Austin Dobson

---

[1] *bards*—a literary, old-fashioned word for poets, especially important, well-known poets
[2] *Pegasus*—a flying horse from ancient Greek mythology
[3] *vagary*—an strange or unpredictable change in ideas or actions
[4] *mountebank*—deceiver
[5] *pulpiteer*—propagandist

1. Which of the following statements **best** summarizes the **main** theme in this poem?

   A. Poetry should rhyme.

   B. Poetry should have a magic that stirs the reader.

   C. Poetry should be about human experience.

   D. Poetry should be about unusual topics that excite the reader.

2. Which of the following words **best** describes the mood of the poem?

   A. Lively

   B. Strained

   C. Celebratory

   D. Triumphant

3. Whom does the speaker of "On the Future of Poetry" address?

   A. Fellow readers

   B. Literary historians

   C. Writers

   D. Poets

4. The poetic technique that is demonstrated in the lines 1 and 2 is

   A. simile

   B. hyperbole

   C. metaphor

   D. personification

5. The phrase "prose-bound community" (line 4) refers to people who

   A. love to read stories

   B. like television talk shows

   C. dislike reading in general

   D. enjoy clubs and other community organizations

6. What is the verse structure of "On the Future of Poetry"?

   A. Quatrains

   B. Sestets

   C. Octaves

   D. Sonnets

7. Which of the following words **most completely** summarizes the speaker's feelings about the future of poetry?

   A. Optimistic

   B. Pessimistic

   C. Ambivalent

   D. Terrified

8. In the context of line 18, the word "blank" refers to words that

   A. rhyme

   B. have a distinct rhythm

   C. are confusing

   D. do not rhyme

Reading Two

From *Eye of the Moon*

Someone had dropped a chocolate-covered ice cream bar in the middle of the sidewalk. Impact with the pavement had flattened it into an off-white oval splat with an irregular brown centre that bled into the creamy mess. The whole thing looked a bit like a sloppy flower, the wooden stick its short stem. Over time the whole thing would grow more murky. Pedestrians on their way to work or to the bus stop, cyclists who insisted on using the sidewalk, joggers like me, all had to make a detour around the splat or jump over. Never once that summer did anyone step into it. When the sun rose the sweet substance attracted an obscene buzz of flies.

The end of the school year always coincided with my birthday and in my seventeenth year it coincided also with my grandmother's corneal implant. … Nineteen tiny, tiny stitches, the eye surgeon told my mother, and five times a day they would have to be lubricated with medicated drops. Like watering a seedling.

I had just finished grade eleven and the plan had been to get a summer job. "No reason she can't help with her university costs," Mother said, thinking of my future, and Dad, who ever since my fifteenth birthday had become convinced that all youth was headed for hell in a hand basket, said, "Won't hurt her one bit to get a feel for work." They had a habit of speaking about me in the third person, as if I wasn't there. Or as if I was deaf. Or still a child. The habit had solidified; maybe the indirectness offered Dad a buffer against the awkwardness of dealing with an adolescent in the volatile process of becoming a woman.

A job was okay with me. Jody and Claire, my closest friends at that time, had found jobs after grade ten, and the benefits of time away from parents and extra money weren't lost on me. I put in applications at Domo Gas and Wendy's and the library, but before anyone wanted me for an interview the hospital called to say a cornea had become available and Nana had to be there right away. ... She was a tough bird, Nana, and within a week she was back in her apartment in the seniors' high rise. The public health nurse would come first thing in the morning, but that left four more applications of eye drops daily for five weeks.

5   Nana, at eighty, kept track of her arthritis medicine, time of day, the changing seasons, birthdays. "I've got all my marbles, thank God," she'd say. But the nurse couldn't get her to squeeze the eyedropper without first shutting her eye, and my mother couldn't change her vacation which she'd booked for September.

"She'll have the rest of her life to work." Dad was looking at me, talking to Mother. "Why does she have to start this summer?"

To be fair, my parents didn't force me into doing the eye drops. They let me choose — a job or Nana. And they would pay me, though not as much as a job, if I chose Nana. If she'd been a complainer and fussy like Dad's mother, I might have balked. But Nana and I got along. It would be a fifteen-minute jog each way. That appealed to me. And I could take the stairs to the sixth floor. Maybe by the time school resumed in fall my body would be in some sort of shape I could maintain for graduation. Besides, the stretches of free time between eye drops held tempting possibilities.

"Weekends you'll be off," Mother said. "That's when your Dad and I will take care of Nana."

The splat on the sidewalk must have been new my first day of duty. It was a morning in late June, the sun brooding redly through the smog that hung above the shopping mall. There was no wind, and I felt sticky. I didn't see the mess staring up at me like a large eye until the last minute and had to take a flying leap over it to save my new runners from getting mucked up. In spite of the heat it felt good to be up and running and I imagined the unwanted flesh melting from my thighs. The chickadees were nervously busy in the trees, kids lounged in front of the Seven Eleven and on the south side of a small white bungalow a cat lay stretched out in the sun.

10   "What are you doing for summer holidays?" Nana asked after I'd made her tip her head way back, then pulled her eyelid up with my thumb the way the nurse had shown me, positioned the dropper correctly above the bloodshot, sutured eye, steadied my hand and squeezed out a tiny globule of liquid that fell more or less on target. I removed my thumb and the wrinkled eyelid fell shut like a china doll's. I dabbed away the moisture pearling from the corner of the eye with a cotton swab and taped gauze over it, proud of myself and relieved I'd actually done it alone for the first time.

"I said, what are you doing this summer, Julia?"

As I said, Nana was pretty sharp, but it hadn't registered that this year, she was my summer. In the beginning I didn't think of myself as locked into a schedule. Starting before ten every day, wind or calm, humidity or unrelenting sun, I would jog at three hour intervals the two blocks down our street, across the highway at Springfield Avenue, then along that winding stretch of the Donwood Drive sidewalk past the brown and white splat to Donwood Manor where Nana lived. The route would be familiar as my own breathing before summer was over, a summer when everything would become desperate for rain.

"There's lots to do in summer, Nana," I said. "Fringe Festival starts next week, I might go. They're doing King Lear."

"Hmm," she said. Nana hadn't read much Shakespeare.

15   No point in telling her that Brendan Gorlick, who had just graduated from River East High and therefore stood on the threshold of the future, was playing the part of the fool or that the tragedy would be condensed—ninety minutes was max for the Fringe. This was all beyond Nana's world.

Last winter Brendan played John Proctor in The Crucible in our school production. He always got big parts and I always got, "Julia, you'll be one of the stage hands, OK?"

"That's important," Brendan would say. "Stage hands are important." His earnestness melted my inexperienced heart. Brendan was kind, and at that point in my life any kindness I encountered made me stop short. It comforted me, as if I'd come home.

A teenager playing John Proctor is bound to be at a disadvantage. I doubt if Brendan had ever grappled with questions of betrayal and integrity any more than I had. But everyone said he'd been great in the role, and now he had a small part in King Lear.

I wasn't expecting Nana to be filled with gratitude every time I came to do the drops. Still, when you think you're making a sacrifice, you want it to be noticed. Nana simply assumed I had come for a long visit. "Leaving already?" she'd say, totally astonished.

20   By the time the Fringe opened, the nurse said Nana's eye was doing fine, keep up the good work, these next weeks would be crucial. The splat on the sidewalk had shrunk a little and I had begun to fantasize running in cool rain. Dad spoke of global warming. "Scientists agree on that. There's evidence. By the time our offspring grows up, who knows." He'd be speaking to Mother, looking sideways at me.

Mother, when she came home from work at five-thirty, went directly to the basement, the coolest place, and spent the evening watching TV. Nobody but Dad felt like eating. "Go ahead, make yourself something. Pasta. Salad," Mother said sipping a cold beer.

The opening of the Fringe was scheduled for Friday, more or less all day. I decided to bike down to Market Square between the ten o'clock and one o'clock drops, not only because Brendan might be there, but because the novelty of the four daily trips to Donwood Manor was beginning to wear thin. Jody and Claire always seemed to be working when I was free and the days of summer vacation were running past without anything happening. That was the summer I first began reflecting on time, how it slips like water through the cracks of the day. How irretrievable it is. As impossible to rewind as to fast forward.

Sarah Klassen

9. Why doesn't Julia get a summer job?

    A. Her parents pay her to look after Nana.

    B. None of the places she applied to phone her for an interview.

    C. Her friends had already taken all the good jobs.

    D. She is too young, and she has the rest of her life to work.

10. Julia's father is characterized as a stereotypical dad in that he

    A. wants Julia to help with university costs

    B. likes to relax in the basement and drink beer

    C. thinks Julia should exercise more

    D. is awkward in dealing with an adolescent girl

11. What literary device is exemplified by the phrase "buzz of flies" (paragraph 1)?

    A. Alliteration

    B. Onomatopoeia

    C. Irony

    D. Symbolism

12. The phrase " 'I've got all my marbles' " (paragraph 5) is an example of

    A. personification

    B. propaganda

    C. simile

    D. metaphor

13. The type of writing that the passage can best be described as is

    A. narrative

    B. satirical

    C. persuasive

    D. argumentative

14. The word "balked" (paragraph 7) can be **best** defined as

    A. rejoiced

    B. refused

    C. agreed

    D. moped

15. For Julia, the benefits of working with Nana include all of the following reasons **except**

    A. earning some money

    B. getting in shape

    C. being able to see more plays

    D. having free time

16. Why is Nana surprised when Julia leaves so quickly?

    A. She doesn't realize that Julia has just come to do her job.

    B. She doesn't understand how important the play is to Julia.

    C. She still needs more help.

    D. She is expecting visitors.

17. Why does Julia begin reflecting on the passage of time?

    A. She sees her Nana aging more quickly.

    B. She realizes that time is impossible to rewind.

    C. She is positive that she won't connect with Brendan.

    D. She realizes that things are going on around her, but she herself isn't doing anything.

18. The phrase "the wrinkled eyelid fell shut like a china doll's" (paragraph 10) is an example of

    A. simile

    B. metaphor

    C. personification

    D. alliteration

19. Which of the following words **best** describes Nana's character?

    A. Hardy

    B. Squeamish

    C. Demanding

    D. Confused

Reading Three

Scientists solve 2,000-year-old mystery of geckos' glue

Geckos stick to walls by exploiting a weak electrical attraction between their feet and the wall, according to new, military-funded research that could change everything from rock climbing to playing football.

The little lizards, among nature's best climbers, can race up walls, across ceilings and hang their entire weight with just one foot on even the smoothest of surfaces. But how their feet stick — whether by glue, grip or something else — has resisted explanation since Aristotle first marveled at them in his *Historia animalium*.

Competing explanations this century suggested some sort of water bond, or even a chemical reaction with the wall surface.

The just-discovered answer is a subatomic electrical attraction, discovered in the 1800s and known as van der Waals force.

5   Kellar Autumn of Lewis and Clark college in Oregon shows in a paper published today that infinitesimal hairs on geckos' feet — each lizard has several million — come in such close contact with the surfaces they climb that individual molecules temporarily change their electrical charge, forming a powerful bond between foot and wall.

The applications of the discovery, while still in the theoretical stage, are intriguing. Dr. Autumn fancies building a gecko-footed robot for exploring Mars but, in the nearer future, a gecko-inspired dry adhesive could be used in various industries: from alignment of fibre-optics and manipulation of tiny silicon computer parts, to something as mundane as an ultrastrong household adhesive.

For the adventurous and the athletic, though, it gets even better — gecko climbing gloves.

In an interview yesterday, Dr. Autumn recalled seeing the recent *Spiderman* movie on a flight, and marvelling at how true to biology it was. In the movie, young Peter Parker grew mysterious hairs on his hands after being bitten by a genetically-modified spider. Suddenly, he could climb vertical walls.

"I was actually thinking that we'd be able to do better some day," Dr. Autumn said, suggesting that gecko hand- and footwear could revolutionize the sport of rock-climbing.

10   "Or you could pick your favourite football team and imagine them never fumbling the ball with their gecko gloves. Safety devices as well," he said.

Spiders have similar hair-like structures on their legs, though it is not known for certain whether they evolved to exploit van der Waals force. It seems likely, however, that spiders and geckos are an example of convergent evolution — the independent evolution of similar traits to solve similar problems in the environment.

"It may very well be that there's this common design picture that evolution keeps arriving at," Dr. Autumn said. "It involves splitting a surface into many smaller pieces to achieve close intimate contact with the surface."

The contact is so intimate that individual molecules in the feet and the wall are brought close enough to change the other's electrical charge. Since similar charges repel and opposites attract, a weak electrical bond is formed each time contact is made. Multiply this van der Waals force by the millions of hairs that manage to achieve it, and you have a powerful electrical glue.

"They sort of do this quantum dance together, and as long as they're close enough, that force can actually be fairly substantial," he said.

15   The tiny hairs are called setae and each one is about 100 micrometres long. Each seta ends with 1,000 tiny pads at its tip – further increasing the contact between foot and wall. Each pad is smaller than the wavelength of light and can only be observed with an electron microscope.

A million setae, which would fit on a dime, could support a child. All the setae on one gecko, if bonded at the same time, could hold up a linebacker.

In reality, though, a gecko only ever manages to successfully bond about one in 3,300 of its setae, which results in a powerful force nonetheless, Dr. Autumn said.

The force is so large, in fact, even from the few successful bonds that the gecko should theoretically be unable to let go. In a paper published two years ago, the same team showed that the key to the gecko's effortless release is the angle of its foot; if it is greater than about 30 degrees, the force is broken and the setae pop off.

This discovery came hand-in-hand with an explanation for how to make the setae stick. "First you must align it precisely in three dimensions," Dr. Autumn said. "Then you must push in with a force of between five and 15 micronewtons, then you must drag towards the rear about five microns. If you do that, you get an astonishingly large adhesive force out of that one seta."

20   Geckos, so named because of the clicking noise some of them make, live in the wild in deserts, rainforests and grasslands, and can now be found worldwide as pets.

Dr. Autumn's research, which was funded in part by the United States' Defense Advanced Research Projects Agency, appears in today's edition of the Proceedings of the National Academy of Sciences.

Joseph Brean

20. The **main** purpose of this article is to

A. explain how geckos' feet stick to surfaces

B. encourage people to think of applications for geckos' glue

C. teach readers about lizards

D. market new kinds of glue

21. Who solved the mystery of how geckos' feet stick to surfaces?

    A. Lewis Clark

    B. Kellar Autumn

    C. Joseph Brean

    D. Aristotle

22. Geckos' feet are able to stick to surfaces as a result of

    A. an electrical attraction

    B. a glue-like substance

    C. a water bond

    D. a chemical reaction

23. Why was Dr. Autumn amazed by the movie *Spiderman*?

    A. His flight was long and arduous.

    B. He was bitten by a genetically modified spider.

    C. The way the character could climb walls has a biological explanation.

    D. The character grows hairs on his body in a biological way.

24. One thing that spiders and lizards possibly have in common is that both

    A. have developed a similar trait to solve an environmental problem

    B. destroy their environment in order to be able to continue evolving

    C. are divergent evolvers

    D. use convergent structures on their legs

25. How are geckos able to remove themselves from walls?

    A. By pushing the setae

    B. By popping their feet up

    C. By angling their feet

    D. By using force

26. What is the most probable reason the United States Defense Advanced Research Projects Agency funded the research?

    A. The research could improve how football is played.

    B. The scientists vowed to work in secret.

    C. The agency hopes to use the findings to facilitate travel to Mars.

    D. The research could have applications for the armed forces.

27. Which of the following terms can be applied to words such as "molecules," "setae," and "micronewtons" in a newspaper article?

    A. False reasoning

    B. Viewpoints

    C. Scientific jargon

    D. Scientific definitions

28. The expression "electrical glue" is an example of the literary device of

    A. personification

    B. metaphor

    C. symbolism

    D. irony

Reading Four

World Cup 1998

This soaring game in which every player
wears concentration like a skin,
his body like Nureyev's[1], flying
higher each time than the next man
5   (he hopes) toward that desperately sought after
firefly, the soccer ball.

France vs. Norway, Brazil vs. Spain,
their bodies speak an old familiar language
of men in action—fierce competition
10   for a symbol, a ball, for anything,
this head-knocking race for mastery and at the end,
a grudging respect
for the pure muscle of it,
the head-cracking, joint-knocking, ball-kicking explosion
15   of strength and skill and even luck they will celebrate later.

But now
it's the purest pleasure of the doing in a race for the best
and men who finally, in this ultimate celebration
of the body
20   can afford to embrace and cry, in love
at last.

                                     Kate Braid

29. Which of the following aspects of the game of soccer is this poem mainly about?

    A. The emotions of the fans

    B. The injuries of the players

    C. The passion of the game

    D. The technique of the athletes

30. The contrast of "men in action — fierce competition" (line 9) with "embrace and cry, in love/at last" (lines 20 to 21) serves to

    A. break a stereotypical image

    B. describe the foolishness of the men

    C. show the high level of play

    D. create suspense

---

[1] Rudolf Nureyev was a famous ballet dancer

31. Which of the following statements **best** describes the theme of the poem?

    A. Soccer is similar in some ways to dancing.

    B. People celebrate with all their might when their country's team wins.

    C. Competition is often aggressive and can cause people to get upset.

    D. When people are passionate about what they do, their emotions soar.

32. The comparison of the soccer player to the ballet dancer suggests that the

    A. player leaps through the air with beauty

    B. player must practice as much as a dancer does

    C. dancer is like an athlete

    D. game of soccer is intricately choreographed

33. The lines "France vs. Norway, Brazil vs. Spain, / their bodies speak an old familiar language" (lines 7 to 8) suggest that

    A. even though the players' native tongues are different, the jargon of soccer is familiar to them all.

    B. the players' speak different languages, but their motivation and actions are the same.

    C. the players are aging and compete fiercely to win the World Cup for their countries.

    D. the action on the field is difficult for the players from different countries to understand..

34. The literary device used in the lines "that desperately sought after / firefly, the soccer ball" (lines 5 to 6) is

    A. simile

    B. metaphor

    C. oxymoron

    D. conflict

35. When the poet refers to the ball as a "symbol" (line 10), she most likely means that the ball is a symbol of

    A. love

    B. power

    C. victory

    D. emotion

PRACTICE EXAMINATION 3

Reading One

You Had Two Girls

You had two girls—Baptiste—
One is Virginie—
Hold hard—Baptiste!
Listen to me.

5 The whole drive was jammed
In that bend at the Cedars,
The rapids were dammed
With the logs tight rammed
And crammed; you might know
10 The Devil had clinched them below.

We worked three days—not a budge,
"She's as tight as a wedge, on the ledge,"
Says our foreman;
"Mon Dieu! boys, look here,
15 We must get this thing clear."
He cursed at the men
And we went for it then;
With our cant-dogs[1] arow,[2]
We just gave he-yo-ho;
20 When she gave a big shove
From above.

The gang yelled and tore
For the shore,
The logs gave a grind
25 Like a wolf's jaws behind,
And as quick as a flash,
With a shove and a crash,
They were down in a mash,
But I and ten more,
30 All but Isaàc Dufour,
Were ashore.

---

[1] *cant dogs*—or cant hooks; short, heavy poles with a spike and a swiveling hook at one end; used to twist a log
[2] *arow*—in a row; a line of men with cant dogs are twisting the logs to free them and loosen the jam

He leaped on a log in the front of the rush,
And shot out from the bind
While the jam roared behind;
35   As he floated along
He balanced his pole
And tossed us a song.
But just as we cheered,
Up darted a log from the bottom,
40   Leaped thirty feet square and fair,
And came down on his own.

He went up like a block
With the shock,
And when he was there
45   In the air,
Kissed his hand
To the land;
When he dropped
My heart stopped,
50   For the first logs had caught him
And crushed him;
When he rose in his place
There was blood on his face.

There were some girls, Baptiste,
55   Picking berries on the hillside,
Where the river curls, Baptiste,
You know—on the still side
One was down by the water,
She saw Isaàc
60   Fall back.

She did not scream, Baptiste,
She launched her canoe;
It did seem, Baptiste,
That she wanted to die too,
65   For before you could think
The birch cracked like a shell
In that rush of hell,
And I saw them both sink—

Baptiste!—
70   He had two girls,
One is Virginie,
What God calls the other
Is not known to me.

Duncan Campbell Scott

1. Which of the following statements **best** describes what happens in the poem?

   A. A man and a woman drown on the river.

   B. A logjam becomes unstuck, but kills a logger and a woman.

   C. The speaker addresses someone named "Baptiste."

   D. Loggers led a dangerous life.

2. The repetition of sounds in the words "jammed," "dammed," "rammed," and "crammed," (verse 2) emphasizes

   A. how tightly the logs were stuck on the river

   B. the sound the logs were making on the river

   C. the speaker's frustration at not getting the logs free for three days

   D. the internal rhyme

3. The speaker states that as Isaàc Dufour "floated along" (line 35), he "tossed us a song" (line 37). The lightness of the verb "tossed" together with the simple rhyme of "along" with "song" contrast with the

   A. horrible sound of the logs grinding behind him

   B. cheers of the men on the shore

   C. silence of the woman in the canoe

   D. tragedy of his drowning an instant later

4. Which of the following words **best** describes the girl?

   A. Hysterical

   B. Careless

   C. Brave

   D. Afraid

5. That the girl's birch canoe "cracked like a shell" (line 66) implies

   A. that the girl should not have followed Dufour into the water

   B. the ease with which the powerful logs snapped her canoe

   C. the ease with which shells tend to crack

   D. that the girl did not know how to paddle in those conditions

6. Who is the narrator of the poem?

    A. One of the loggers

    B. Virginie

    C. The father

    D. Isaàc Dufour

7. The most likely reason that the speaker does not name the second girl is that she

    A. was the braver of the two sisters

    B. is the one who drowned

    C. never told him her name before she went out in her canoe

    D. did not even know how to swim

Reading Two

From *Eve's Ransom*

An hour later he was at Old Square, waiting for the tram to Aston. Huge   steam-driven vehicles came and went, whirling about the open space with monitory bell-clang. Amid a press of homeward-going workfolk, Hilliard clambered to a place on the top and lit his pipe. He did not look the same man who had waited gloomily at Dudley Port; his eyes gleamed with life; answering a remark addressed to him by a neighbour on the car, he spoke jovially.

No rain was falling, but the streets shone wet and muddy under lurid lamp-lights. Just above the house-tops appeared the full moon, a reddish disk, blurred athwart floating vapour. The car drove northward, speedily passing from the region of main streets and great edifices into a squalid district of factories and workshops and crowded by-ways. At Aston Church the young man alighted, and walked rapidly for five minutes, till he reached a row of small modern houses. Socially they represented a step or two upwards in the gradation which, at Birmingham, begins with the numbered court and culminates in the mansions of Edgbaston.

He knocked at a door, and was answered by a girl, who nodded recognition.

"Mrs. Hilliard in? Just tell her I'm here."

5   There was a natural abruptness in his voice, but it had a kindly note, and a pleasant smile accompanied it. After a brief delay he received permission to go upstairs, where the door of a sitting-room stood open. Within was a young woman, slight, pale, and pretty, who showed something of embarrassment, though her face made him welcome.

"I expected you sooner."

"Business kept me back. Well, my niece?"

The table was spread for tea, and at one end of it, on a high chair, sat a child of four years old. Hilliard kissed her, and stroked her curly hair, and talked with playful affection. This little girl was his niece, the child of his elder brother, who had died three years ago. The poorly furnished room and her own attire proved that Mrs. Hilliard had but narrow resources in her widowhood. Nor did she appear a woman of much courage; tears had thinned her cheeks, and her delicate hands had suffered noticeably from unwonted household work.

Hilliard remarked something unusual in her behaviour this evening. She was restless, and kept regarding him askance, as if in apprehension. A letter from her, in which she merely said she wished to speak to him, had summoned him hither from Dudley. As a rule, they saw each other but once a month.

10   "No bad news, I hope!" he remarked aside to her, as he took his place at the table.

"Oh, no. I'll tell you afterwards."

Very soon after the meal Mrs. Hilliard took the child away and put her to bed. During her absence the visitor sat brooding, a peculiar half-smile on his face. She came back, drew a chair up to the fire, but did not sit down.

"Well, what is it?" asked her brother-in-law, much as he might have spoken to the little girl.

"I have something very serious to talk about, Maurice."

15 "Have you? All right; go ahead."

"I—I am so very much afraid I shall offend you."

The young man laughed.

"Not very likely. I can take a good deal from you."

She stood with her hands on the back of the chair, and as he looked at her, Hilliard saw her pale cheeks grow warm.

20 "It'll seem very strange to you, Maurice."

"Nothing will seem strange after an adventure I've had this afternoon. You shall hear about it presently."

"Tell me your story first."

"All right, I'll tell you. I met that scoundrel Dengate, and—he's paid me the money he owed my father."

"He has *paid* it? Oh! really?"

25 "See, here's a cheque, and I think it likely I can turn it into cash. The blackguard has been doing well at Liverpool. I'm not quite sure that I understand the reptile, but he seems to have given me this because I abused him. I hurt his vanity, and he couldn't resist the temptation to astonish me. He thinks I shall go about proclaiming him a noble fellow. Four hundred and thirty-six pounds[1]; there it is."

He tossed the piece of paper into the air with boyish glee, and only just caught it as it was fluttering into the fire.

"Oh, be careful!" cried Mrs. Hilliard.

"I told him he was a scoundrel, and he began by threatening to thrash me. I'm very glad he didn't try. It was in the train, and I know very well I should have strangled him. It would have been awkward, you know."

"Oh, Maurice, how *can* you——?"

30 "Well, here's the money; and half of it is yours."

"Mine? Oh, no! After all you have given me. Besides, I sha'n't[2] want it."

"How's that?"

---

[1] *four hundred and thirty-six pounds*—at that time, a large sum of money; skilled workers made less than a hundred pounds a year

[2] *Sha'n't*—shan't; contraction of *shall not*; the spelling was correct when the story was written

Their eyes met. Hilliard again saw the flush in her cheeks, and began to guess its explanation. He looked puzzled, interested.

"Do I know him?" was his next inquiry.

35   "Should you think it very wrong of me?" She moved aside from the line of his gaze. "I couldn't imagine how you would take it."

"It all depends. Who is the man?"

Still shrinking towards a position where Hilliard could not easily observe her, the young widow told her story. She had consented to marry a man of whom her brother-in-law knew little but the name, one Ezra Marr; he was turned forty, a widower without children, and belonged to a class of employers of labour. The contrast between such a man and Maurice Hilliard's brother was sufficiently pronounced; but the widow nervously did her best to show Ezra Marr in a favourable light.

"And then," she added after a pause, while Hilliard was reflecting, "I couldn't go on being a burden on you. How very few men would have done what you have—"

"Stop a minute. Is *that* the real reason? If so—"

40   Hurriedly she interposed.

"That was only one of the reasons—only one."

Hilliard knew very well that her marriage had not been entirely successful; it seemed to him very probable that with a husband of the artisan class, a vigorous and go-ahead fellow, she would be better mated than in the former instance. He felt sorry for his niece, but there again sentiment doubtless conflicted with common-sense. A few more questions, and it became clear to him that he had no ground of resistance.

"Very well. Most likely you are doing a wise thing. And half this money is yours; you'll find it useful."

George Gissing

8. The relationship between Maurice and Mrs. Hilliard can best be described as

   A. comfortable

   B. intimate

   C. distant

   D. tense

9. The reason that Hilliard "did not look the same man who had waited gloomily at Dudley Port" (paragraph 1) was that since then,

   A. he had been paid money that was owed to him.

   B. he had been paid money that was owed to his father.

   C. 436 pounds had been paid to his father.

   D. his niece had invited him over for dinner.

10. By having Hilliard call Dengate a "reptile" (paragraph 25), the writer is employing the literary technique of

    A. simile

    B. hyperbole

    C. metaphor

    D. personification

11. The reason that Maurice claims to be glad Dengate did not try to thrash him in the train is that

    A. everyone would have seen Maurice get a beating.

    B. Maurice would have had nowhere to run.

    C. Maurice could not have gotten the money from Dengate.

    D. Maurice would have strangled Dengate with everyone watching.

12. Which is the following statements **best** explains Mrs. Hilliard's invitation to Maurice?

    A. She had just been paid 436 pounds.

    B. She was getting married to Ezra Marr.

    C. She was eloping with Ezra Marr.

    D. She had some strange news to tell Maurice.

13. The **main** reason that Mrs. Hilliard will not take half of Maurice's money despite his offer
is that

    A. he has already done so much for her.

    B. she would rather have his affections.

    C. she no longer actually needs the money.

    D. he does not really intend to give it to her.

14. In context, the phrase "no ground of resistance" (paragraph 42) **most probably** means that
Hilliard

    A. could not resist her approach

    B. felt he was losing ground to her

    C. needed to stand his ground

    D. had no reason to object

Reading Three

Schools use daily gym class in battle with child obesity

Schools across the country are fighting the epidemic of childhood obesity by scheduling a
daily gym class, even if it means doing exercises in a regular classroom.

No longer willing to wait for direction from provincial education ministries, a handful of
school administrators have found time in their packed curriculums for an organized
period of running, skipping or playing ball five days a week.

Fewer than 200 schools across the country have accomplished the scheduling feat, but the
national physical education association that keeps track says it has already received 1,000
applications for its 2004 Quality Daily Physical Education awards.

It took teachers at Wilson Middle School in Lethbridge, Alta., 30 tries before they came
up with a daily schedule that includes one period of gym for each of their 600 students in
Grades 6, 7 and 8.

5   One day a week the school has four phys. ed. classes going at the same time — two in the
gym, one on the school stage and another in a smaller fitness room.

"We had to do something," says Rod Dueck, the assistant vice-principal and part-time
gym teacher. "They go home and sit on the couch and play Xbox and snack on chips.
It's an epidemic."

Last year, Statistics Canada reported that 37% of Canadian children aged 2 through 11
are overweight, with half of that number considered obese.

The new daily gym classes at the Lethbridge school emphasize participation rather than
competition, focusing on games such as tag or capture the flag instead of basketball to
ensure everyone is running around.

Fourteen-year-old Brittany Toth admits her classmates sometimes grumble about the daily putting on and taking-off of sneakers and sweat pants, but most have starting viewing gym as the best part of the school day. Another result is that the boys and girls are no longer separated during gym class. "That makes it even more fun," Brittany says. "We have to try harder."

10   Mr. Dueck, a life-long athlete who grew his muscles doing chores on the family farm, says he has learned to dream up ways to encourage the awkward, shy members of his classes to get off the sidelines and participate. Lethbridge's three public middle schools abbreviated their competitive sport seasons so more students would come out after school and play soccer and volleyball without fear of getting cut from the team. Upwards of 150 students are turning up after school for sports.

"At this age, it's devastating for a kid to not make a team," said Mr. Dueck. "You end up cutting kids in middle school when their bodies are growing, and by the time they get to high school, they could have developed into great athletes, but they never got the chance."

The southern Alberta school stopped selling soft drinks, chocolates and fried foods in its cafeteria in September, months in advance of this week's announcement by Coca-Cola and Pepsi pledging to withdraw carbonated beverages from elementary and middle schools across the country before the next school year.

Education ministers in Alberta, British Columbia and Quebec have pondered requiring daily gym classes as a solution to the obesity problem, but none has announced any policy changes so far. A B.C. proposal to make students in Grades 11 and 12 take at least one gym course a year was dropped out of fear it would take time away from academics.

In Ontario, physical education is required only three times a week in Grades 1 through 8. Just one credit in gym is required to graduate high school.

15   But principals such as Mignonne Wood of Lakeview Elementary School in Burnaby, B.C., say physical education can be increased without extending the school day or hiring addition al instructors if teachers and administrators are willing to be creative with their schedules.

On Mondays, to ensure everyone has some time in the gym, the students warm up in their classrooms and walk in the hallways to cool down after exercising for 20 minutes.

The suburban school began offering daily gym this year, even though the   250-student, kindergarten through Grade 7 campus has no physical education specialists on staff. Classroom teachers lead the students in daily exercises and games. Officials at Burnaby's school board want all schools in the district to follow suit.

Heather Sokoloff

15. The reason that schools are trying to fit in more physical education classes is that

    A. students need to try harder and become more competitive in life.

    B. students are not active enough and are becoming more obese.

    C. the schools need to make better use of space.

    D. too many students go home and play video games.

16. According to Mr. Dueck, a negative result of cutting middle school children from sports teams is that it

    A. forces them to deal with rejection at too young of an age

    B. teaches them that they have poor athletic skills

    C. fosters obesity in youth

    D. takes away an opportunity for them to become good athletes

17. What does the use of the words "only" and "just" in paragraph 14 tell us about the article?

    A. Many people have been interviewed for the article.

    B. There is bias.

    C. There is no bias.

    D. The system in Ontario is not very good.

18. Lakeview Elementary was able to offer daily gym classes by

    A. making the school day longer

    B. adding more teachers to the staff

    C. having principals and vice-principals teach the gym classes

    D. changing the schedule

Although the next two readings appear to be quite different, both are about art (visual art and musical art). What similarities do you notice?

Reading Four

How much can music influence your feelings?

When to Her Lute Corinna Sings

When to her lute[1] Corinna sings,
Her voice revives the leaden strings,
And doth[2] in highest notes appear,
As any challenged echo clear;
5   But when she doth of mourning speak,
Even with her sighs the strings do break.

And as her lute doth live or die,
Led by her passion, so must I,
For when of pleasure she doth sing,
10   My thoughts enjoy a sudden spring,
But if she doth of sorrow speak,
Even from my heart the strings do break.

Thomas Campion

19. Which of the following statements gives the main idea of the poem?

    A. A singer's audience can be challenging.

    B. Music can stir deep emotions in people.

    C. Instruments can easily fall into disrepair.

    D. Life and death are like sorrowful songs.

20. The phrase "Her voice revives the leaden strings" (line 2) refers to how

    A. the lute strings are on the verge of dying

    B. beautifully Corinna plays the lute

    C. beautiful the lute looks once it is revived

    D. the strings echo Corinna's voice when she sings

---

[1] *lute*—a musical instrument like a guitar, but with a pear-shaped body and often a long neck
[2] *doth*—does; in Campion's day, the verb *do*, when used as an auxiliary, or helping, verb, had these different forms: I *do*, thou *dost*, she *doth*, I *did*, thou *didst*, she *did*; thus, Campion would write *she doth sing*

21. The line "And as her lute does live or die" (line 7) is an example of the poetic technique of

    A. oxymoron

    B. metaphor

    C. hyperbole

    D. personification

22. When the speaker states that his thoughts "enjoy a sudden spring" (line 10), he **most probably** means that

    A. his thoughts spring up

    B. his mind comes to life

    C. he feels as if he is drinking from a spring

    D. he feels as if his mind is bouncing like a spring

23. Between the first stanza and the second stanza, a shift occurs from

    A. the speaker's description of the singing to its effect on his own heart

    B. the speaker's description of Corinna's heart to her lute strings

    C. Corinna's description of her singing to her speaking

    D. a second-person narrator to a first-person narrator

24. According to the speaker, when Corinna sings, she sings about pleasure. When she speaks, she speak about

    A. unhappiness

    B. music

    C. sorrow

    D. her lute

25. The poet has written this poem using

    A. rhyming couplets

    B. free verse

    C. blank verse

    D. quatrains

Reading Five

Where the Reids Lived

I never plan art gallery visits; they just happen one day as I am walking past. To paraphrase Forrest Gump's mother: "An art gallery is like a box of chocolates. You never know what you're going to get." There is no need for me to know in advance all I will see. And so it was when I went in about a year ago, when the sign said: "The Group of Seven in Western Canada."

I am greeted by Lawren Harris's Mountain Forms – the image sharp, clean, cold, tall, angular. Where was he standing, I wonder, when he saw the Rockies that way? I have lived near Jasper, Alta. I have seen them as he did.

Frederick Varley is shown in a tiny room with a beautiful stained glass window. I am interested to see a portrait in the grouping, and more interested to learn that the model and the artist were said to be an item. I am pleased and surprised to find, in the next room, that two of the Seven painted abstract pieces. Oh, but I am enjoying myself!

Arthur Lismer's Cathedral Mountain, when I find it, is large and strong. I do not see Cathedral Mountain as he obviously did. Still, it evokes for me visits to nearby Lake Louise when the poppies are in bloom and the lake is so clear and green it can not possibly be real.

5   Harris, J.E.H. MacDonald, A.Y. Jackson. And then, suddenly, there it is. I knew it existed but I had never seen it "live." Doc Snyder's House, L.L. FitzGerald. I can feel the G force as the time machine hurls me back 49 years. It wasn't Doc Snyder's house then – it was mine. I was 10. There is the bedroom window I climbed out to gain access to the porch roof, from where I hoped to see into FitzGerald's yard. I did not go unnoticed, and a lecture ensued about the dangers of climbing out of upstairs windows, not to mention respecting people's privacy. Mother was not amused.

There is the fence, much taller than I was, that I scrutinized for knotholes through which I might see what a real artist looked like. How mysterious and forbidden the FitzGerald garden had seemed.

There were hardwood floors in Doc Snyder's house, my house, and a huge hot air register in the middle of the main floor – between the dining room and the living room. I would stand on it on cold Winnipeg winter mornings, and feel the warm draft up my billowing, flannel nightgown. I could smell the wet wool mittens shrinking on the grid where we placed them to dry after sessions of tobogganing down the banks of the Assiniboine River or skating on it. How tall the house looks against the barren trees and cold Manitoba sky.

There is the edge of Patsy's house next door. It had been wonderful to find that there was a girl just my age! The street had a different name then. It was Oakdale Place and not Deer Lodge Place. There was no identifying plaque on the lawn of Doc Snyder's House. It was simply where the Reids lived.

A lot had changed between 1931, when FitzGerald looked out of his side window one cold winter day and decided to paint his neighbour's house, and 1953, when a family with five kids moved in. A lot has changed since then. The 10-year-old whose fondest wish, besides catching a glimpse of FitzGerald at work, was to learn how to stop on ice skates, is long gone. And where, I wonder, is Patsy?

10 The low murmur of voices in the next gallery activates the switch on the time machine and I am back, not sure how long I have been away. I am standing in the Nova Scotia Art Gallery. There are more paintings, Maud Lewis and others, but I don't want to see them today. I will come again, though, the next time the gallery beckons.

Mary Bowen

26. The fact that the writer doesn't see Cathedral Mountain or her old house as the artists tell us that she

    A. has a different point of view

    B. has matured and is now more critical

    C. does not appreciate paintings

    D. is unable to understand the art

27. As a young girl, the writer thought that the artist next door was

    A. intimidating

    B. intriguing

    C. talented

    D. aloof

28. The description of the house in paragraph 7 contain many examples of

    A. viewpoints

    B. stereotypes

    C. foreshadowing

    D. imagery

29. The predominant tone of this passage is

    A. amused

    B. nostalgic

    C. sympathetic

    D. melodramatic

30. Which of the following statements provides the purpose of the metaphor of the time machine?

    A. It shows how quickly the writer's mind moves to different times and places in her life.

    B. It demonstrates the significance and importance of the past.

    C. It explains how she is able to recall the details of her old house.

    D. It creates a contrast between the different places.

31. Which of the following words best describes the writer's style?

    A. Antiquated

    B. Elevated

    C. Emotive

    D. Formal

Connections

Refer to "When to Her Lute Corinna Sings" and "Where the Reids Lived" to answer questions 32 and 33.

32. Which of the following statements presents an idea that is common to both passages?

    A. Art is intimidating.

    B. Art has the ability to take people away.

    C. The artist is more important than the viewer/listener.

    D. The viewer/listener must pay close attention to be able to appreciate a piece.

33. A feeling that is shared by both the speaker in "When to Her Lute Corinna Sings" and the writer in "Where the Reids lived" is

    A. jealousy

    B. depression

    C. enjoyment

    D. jubilation

ANSWERS AND SOLUTIONS –
PRACTICE EXAMINATION 1

1. D	8. A	15. B	22. A	29. A
2. D	9. D	16. D	23. D	30. A
3. D	10. D	17. C	24. A	31. D
4. A	11. C	18. A	25. D	32. B
5. C	12. D	19. A	26. B	33. A
6. A	13. B	20. C	27. C	34. A
7. B	14. C	21. A	28. D	35. B

Reading One

from *Emma*
Jane Austen

1. D

From paragraph 4 on, the passage describes the change in Emma's life, and it describes Emma's reaction to them. "How was she to bear the change?" (paragraph 7). The main idea is that *it is sometimes difficult to bear life's changes.*

A. Miss Taylor has not deserted Emma; she has moved away because she has married. Some people might regard such a change as desertion, but Emma is too sensible for that. In fact, Emma has "promoted the match" (paragraph 6). She has encouraged her friend to marry.

B. Miss Taylor was the governess—an employee—and she became a friend. However, her being a governess is mentioned only briefly in paragraphs 2 and 3. The fact of her being a friend is fully described in several paragraphs. It is the friendship that is important, not the "nominal office of governess" (paragraph 3).

C. Emma's father "could not meet her in conversation" because he had no particular abilities or talents, and had never done anything. However, "she dearly loved her father" (paragraph 7), so the vague phrase *do not relate well* does not apply.

2. D

In paragraph 4, the "the real evils" are described: Emma has had her own way too much and she thinks too much of herself. (The word *evil* might seem strong, it might even seem to be hyperbole. Today, many people would regard these evils as independence, empowerment, and self-esteem. However, Jane Austen was a sharp-eyed observer of society and behaviour; she knew what indulgence and conceit can lead to).

A. Emma does live in the countryside, but that fact is not mentioned in this excerpt from the novel.

B. Emma's mother had died young, but her place had been taken the excellent Miss Taylor.

C. There is no mention of any need of protection.

3. D

The last sentence of the first paragraph gives Emma's age as nearly twenty-one. Although the sentence indicates that Emma was *nearly* twenty-one years of age, this answer is closer to any of the others.

4. A

Since Miss Taylor was "less … a governess than a friend" (paragraph 3), we can say that she was not really a governess. Then, *governess in name only* fits the context best. She would still be called the governess, but she was really something else.

B. To *nominate* means to put forward someone's name for election or appointment. Also, to *nominate* is an infinitive and *nominal* is clearly an adjective.

C. *Costly* means expensive. There is nothing in the context to suggest any connection to Miss Taylor's salary.

D. Nominal can mean insignificant—*We charge a nominal fee of one dollar*—and since Miss Taylor was less a governess than a friend, her nominal office of governess could mean *insignificant*. However, Miss Taylor's position was very important to Emma; it is just that her position was not really that of governess.

5. C

It is Miss Taylor's marriage and move to a new home that Emma finds difficult to bear. "How was she to bear the change?—It was true that her friend was going only half a mile from them; but Emma was aware that great must be the difference between a Mrs. Weston, only half a mile from them, and a Miss Taylor in the house" (paragraph 7).

A. Isabella, Emma's sister, has married some time before (paragraphs 2 and 6). The change is something that has happened just as the story opens.

B. Emma will still be able to visit. The difficulty is that Miss Taylor is now Mrs. Weston and lives in another house. The situation has changed.

D. Miss Taylor, the governess, has married Mr. Weston, not Emma's father.

6. A

Mr. Weston was "a man of unexceptionable character, easy fortune, suitable age, and pleasant manners…" (paragraph 6). *Easy fortune* means well-to-do. *Unexceptional character* means good character (good character was considered the rule and bad qualities were the exception); and *pleasant manners* suggest that he was easy to get along with—both close enough to *easy-going*.

B. *Pleasant manners* rules out *irritable*. *Unexceptional character* rules out *high-strung*.

C. *Unexceptional character* rules out *lazy*.

D. Living half a mile away would be an advantage from Emma's point of view, but it has nothing to do with Weston's character.

7. B

"Between them it was more the intimacy of sisters" (paragraph 3). Then, *sisterly* describes their friendship.

A. Miss Taylor was close to both daughters (paragraph 3). The point is that she was particularly close to Emma.

C. The loss that Emma feels makes it clear that their friendship was not deteriorating, even though Miss Taylor was leaving. In fact, Emma is glad that she helped Miss Taylor to make a match with Mr. Weston.

D. Since Emma is glad that she helped Miss Taylor to make a match with Mr. Weston and since she reflects that the "event had every promise of happiness for her friend" (paragraph 6), Emma cannot be called self-serving. Nor can Miss Taylor: paragraph 6 describes in detail just how much Emma owed to her friend.

Reading Two

"Stars"
Marjorie Pickthall

8. A

The poem describes the speaker's experience of nature. This experience is the subject of the poem.

B. The statement is true, but it has nothing to do with the poet's response to nature. The fact is not even mentioned.

C. Many of the constellations are named after characters in Greek mythology.

D. There is no suggestion of the calming of fears, only the suggestion that the poet looks at the vastness of the heavens unafraid.

9. D

The first four lines in each stanza have an *abab* rhyming pattern. Then each stanza ends with a rhyming couplet, *cc*. The rhyme scheme is *ababcc*.

10. D

Personification is used to bring out some quality in the thing that is personified. By giving human attributes of movement, grace, and beauty to the stars, the poet expresses what she feels when she looks into the heavens. The personification illustrates the grace and majesty of the constellations as they move across the sky.

A. The stars are not really like human beings at all. The personification is merely a poetic device that is used to express certain emotions. It is not a means of making real comparisons.

B. The slow movement of the stars is personified in the phrases "even pace and slow" and "stately-moving." However, this does not explain the purpose of their personification.

C. A *metaphor* is used to present the stars as shining lights: "Calm lamps within the distant southern sky." Also, it is other stars, not the two constellations, that are compared with lamps.

11. C

The moon lies low in the western sky. We can infer that the moon is about to set.

A. *Not in a vertical position* probably means *not overhead*. While true, this statement is not as accurate as *about to set*.

B. The moon is not full. *Slender* indicates a crescent moon.

D. The words *slender moon* show that the moon is *either* waxing or waning. However, it is not possible to tell which. (Strictly speaking, star charts, together with clues in the poem, could be used to work out the phase of the moon. But it is not possible to tell from the poem alone.)

12. D

Every image in the poem is *seen*. There is nothing to appeal to smell, touch, or taste. The one mention of *singing* is not an example of imagery at all; it is an allusion. The stars are those that sang *when earth was made*—they are not singing now. An *allusion* is an indirect reference to something else, often a literary, religious, historical, or mythological subject. (This allusion is to the Book of Job in the Bible.)

Reading Three

Closet of the Future Picks Out Clothes
Hans Greimel

13. B

The article is full of interesting bits of information about new high-tech products. Its most likely purpose is to entertain readers with what-will-they-think-of-next descriptions of new electronics.

A and D. Both responses are about sales. However, at the time of writing, none of the products was or would be available for several years. In addition, this English-language article is aimed at North Americans, and the products will be available only in Japan. It will be a long time before the readers will be able to buy such things. Marketing is not a likely purpose of the article.

C. Only a few lines contain information about life in Japan. Most of the article is about gee-whiz electronics.

14. C

" 'These are ideas that in a few years we'll be able in some way to sell' " (paragraph 5). Notice that the companies do not have anything ready to sell at the moment. They are just making sure that people are interested and ready to buy in the future. The best answer is *to advertise their products*.

A and D. Since the companies' interest is in future sales, their interest in informing or educating the public is limited to advertisement. Their displays are not public service announcements.

B. There are no sales to stimulate. At the time of writing, sales are years in the future.

15. B

Only one answer has any support in the article: most of the products are designed to make cramped Japanese houses more comfortable (paragraphs 1, 7, and 8).

A. Innovation awards are not mentioned.

C. Making Japan more efficient is not mentioned. In fact, the electronics are meant for comfort, not efficiency.

D. Not only is making houses larger and warmer not mentioned, the new electronics would not affect the size of houses and warmth of houses in any way.

16. D

Since Japanese houses are small, Japanese washing machines are small, and most Japanese households do not have dryers, a combination dryer and washer would likely be beneficial (lines 44–49).

A. *Outside* is only mentioned because most Japanese hang clothes outside to dry.

B. At present, the average washer is half the size of an American dryer. The size of the new combination washer and dryer is not mentioned. (Yet considering the size of Japanese houses, the new machines are probably not that big.)

C. Most people in Japan already have washers.

17. C

All the information about the high-tech toilets is found in paragraphs 3, 8 and 16. A toilet that tests urine to measure blood sugar, protein, and body fat, and sends suspicious results to a doctor over the Internet would detect health problems.

A. Toilet size is not mentioned.

B. The mirror gives skin advice.

D. Lights switch on when a room is entered.

18. A

The refrigerator (paragraph 14) uses a camera link to beam pictures to a mobile phone, and the mirror (paragraph 18) takes infrared pictures of hair and skin.

B. The closet just gives advice based on weather forecasts.

C. The table merely includes a television.

D. The washer only dries the clothes when it has finished washing.

19. A

Adjusting to match people's tastes is the only answer that has support in the article. The mansion has a "computer system that changes…digital artwork to march visitor preferences" (paragraph 20).

B, C, and **D.** The single, brief paragraph on Gates' mansion does not support the other three responses.

Reading Four

Table 4: Percentage of Internet users . . .

When reading charts and graphs, it is often helpful to use a ruler or the edge of a piece of paper to guide the eye across columns or down rows. Mistakes often happen when the eye wanders.

20. C

The table has a title: "Table 4." Of course, even without the title, the format of tables, charts, and graphs should be very familiar.

A, B, and **C.** Recall that line graphs include a line that joins points; bar graphs show quantities with vertical or horizontal bars (or sometimes lines); and pie charts (or pie graphs) are circular, with pie-shaped sections showing amounts.

21. A

The table simply presents information that shows how the Internet is used.

B, C, and **D.** The table contains only information. There is no interpretation, no suggestion, and no promotion. The reader must make any conclusions.

22. A

This question can be answered by examining the figures for Canada as a whole or by examining the figures for each of the provinces. The second method will show any variation by province or by region.

In fact, using either method, email use is the most popular.

B. *Purchased goods or services* has a low Internet use in Canada and in each province.

C. *Information about goods and services* has the second highest Internet use in Canada and in each province.

D. *News sites* have the third highest Internet use in Canada and in each province except for Newfoundland, Prince Edward Island, and Saskatchewan.

23. D

A glance down the *E-banking* column reveals the smallest percentage to be 16.3 (in Saskatchewan).

24. A

You must look under *Purchased goods or services* to find the amount of on-line shopping. British Columbia had the highest percentage: 26.2.

25. D

The top of the "total users" column shows that the numbers given are *000s*, or *thousands*. The number given must be multiplied by 1000. The total number of users in Quebec is 2 723 000 (2 723 × 1 000).

Reading Five

"Pantoum for a Mother in Nunavut"
Claire Battershill

26. B

Each stanza speaks of the mother not fitting in. Everything is strange; she is foreign. She dreams of another place. Being away from home is what the poem is mainly about.

A and D. These are both details included in one stanza or another, but neither of them is what the poem is mainly about. The details are used to develop the main idea.

C. This detail is not included in the poem. It is the mother who is on the telephone. She could be speaking to anyone.

27. C

Look at the quotation in context: "Even in the dingy hotel room, you can't be alone." Also, consider the phrases "small-town gossip follows you everywhere," and "their voices carry for miles." It is clear that she knows that people are gossiping about her everywhere she goes and that the natives are talking about her for miles around.

A. Meetings are not mentioned. Perhaps the laptop and briefcase suggest someone who has many meetings, but that would be an unsupported guess.

B. The foxes are being hunted. *They* can hardly be the reason the woman cannot be alone.

D. Anxiety—worry, fear, foreboding—is not mentioned in this poem. It is not her worries that do not let her be alone.

28. D

Naïve means lacking in experience and judgement. The mother didn't know how cold it would be. With her thin gloves, she is unprepared.

A. There is no mention of gloves being left. She has the gloves with her, not at home.

B. Her work is not mentioned.

C. It might be difficult to figure out the meaning of *naïve* from context. If it meant "expensive", the sentence would still make sense. However, all the images suggest unpreparedness. The gloves are thin. They are unsuitable for the cold north. A word that means "inexperienced" fits better.

29. A

There are several references to the mother being an outsider, thus her loneliness likely stems from feeling out of place.

B. Missing the cherry blossoms is only one sign of her being out of place.

C. We do not know if she actually uses her laptop.

D. Phoning home is a symptom of her loneliness. There is no way to tell how often she phones.

30. A

Imagery is language that appeals to the senses. This line appeals directly to the sense of smell. The image also suggests all the things that are associated with west-coast weather.

B. A literary *paradox* is a statement that seems to be nonsensical or contradictory, but actually expresses truth.

C. *Personification* is the attribution of human characteristics to inanimate objects or to abstract ideas. Sometimes animals are personified.

D. *Oxymoron* is similar to paradox. An oxymoron is the juxtaposition of contradictory words.

31. D

When she is "dreaming of cotton and silk," the mother is wishing she could be wearing lighter clothes and, therefore, could be somewhere else.

A. The fox hunting might make the mother wish that she was elsewhere. Being a city-dweller, she *might* be opposed to hunting (although there is no evidence if this). However, this would be a *cause* of her wanting to be elsewhere. It would not reveal *that* she wants to be elsewhere.

B. "Your hair still smells of west-coast weather" is a poetic way of saying that everything about her belongs somewhere else. Her hair is not that way because she wants to be somewhere else.

C. The embroidered wolves are part of all the strangeness that makes her feel out of place.

32. B

"The telephone is your only escape, / on the other end of the line there is warmth." (lines 15-16) She escapes by phoning people that she knows.

A. The briefcase is only mentioned because it is one more thing that makes her foreign.

C. The natives hunt fox; the mother does not.

D. In the last line, she dreams of cotton and silk; she dreams that she is elsewhere. She does not return to Victoria.

33. A

Alienation is the feeling of being cut off from other people, the feeling of not being part of what is going on. There are several references to the mother being different, an outsider. She feels alienated.

B. The mother is not *impatient*; she is not annoyed or angry.

C. The mother is not *overburdened*. She is not excessively burdened with work or cares.

D. The mother is not *anxious*. She is not nervous, worried, afraid, or concerned about what might happen.

34. A

There is warmth / is soft, like cherry blossoms… The comparison of the cherry blossoms with a warm Victoria spring contains the word *like*; thus it is a simile.

B. A *metaphor* makes a comparison without using like or as. *The warmth is a soft cherry blossom* is a metaphor.

C. An *oxymoron* is not a comparison. *The icy warmth of his smile* contains an example of an oxymoron. Warmth is not icy, but the contradiction in *icy warmth* briefly describes the true feelings hidden behind a show of warmth.

D. *Hyperbole* is exaggeration for effect. *You have had endless warnings.*

35. B

The tone, which is the writer's attitude toward the subject, can best be described as gentle. There is no harshness or unpleasantness of any kind. The situation described is sad, but there is no blaming of the outsider mother or of the local people.

A. The tone is *serious* in the sense of not being funny, or of being calm and thoughtful. However, the *serious* does not describe the tone as fully as *gentle* does.

C. There is no wrongdoing to forgive.

D. *Sarcasm* is saying the opposite of what is really meant, while using an unpleasant tone of voice that makes the real meaning clear. Sarcasm is unpleasant and intended to be hurtful. There is no hint of sarcasm in this poem.

ANSWERS AND SOLUTIONS – PRACTICE EXAMINATION 2

1. C	8. D	15. C	22. A	29. C
2. A	9. A	16. A	23. C	30. A
3. D	10. D	17. D	24. A	31. D
4. C	11. B	18. A	25. C	32. A
5. A	12. D	19. A	26. D	33. B
6. A	13. A	20. A	27. C	34. B
7. A	14. B	21. C	28. B	35. C

Reading One

"On the Future of Poetry"
Henry Austin Dobson

1. C

According to lines 29 and 30, poetry's "first theme is Human Life, / Its hopes and fears, its love and strife"—in other words, poetry should be about human experience.

A. Although the poem itself rhymes, the poet states that poetry either with or without rhyme can be effective. Thus, rhyme is not necessary.

B. Line 5 asks what magic the poets of the future will use to stir the reader, but this (and all the questions in the first part of the poem) are answered "I know not" (line 13). The questions are dropped in favour of what the poet *does* know for certain (lines 17–32). In the second part of the poem, the poet states what poetry *should* be.

D. The poem does not mention *unusual topics that excite the reader*.

2. A

Try reading the poem aloud and listen to the rhythm. Notice that the poem is made up of rhyming couplets. The rhythm, the rhyme, and also the references to music give this poem a lively feeling.

B. *Strained* can mean showing great stress or forced, not spontaneous. Reading aloud will show that neither definition fits. The poem has an easy, natural rhythm; it does not show stress.

C. The poem asks about the future of poetry and then describes the nature of poetry. There is no celebration.

D. Triumphant means showing pride and happiness after a victory, but there is no victory or triumph in this poem.

3. D

It might seem reasonable to assume that the writer of a poem about the future of poetry could be addressing readers, writers, literary historians, *and* poets. However, since the first line of the poem states: "Bards of the future!" the best response is simply *poets*.

4. C

The phrase "… you that come / with striding march, and roll of drum" is an example of *metaphor*, a comparison between two things or a transfer of ideas associated with one object to another. In this case, poets are compared to marchers in a parade.

A. A *simile* is like a metaphor, but it uses *like* or *as* to make the comparison.

B. *Hyperbole* is exaggeration for effect.

D. *Personification* gives human qualities to abstract ideas or to inanimate objects.

5. A

Prose is all the writing that does not include poetry. Since *prose-bound* means *limited to prose*, then the prose-bound community must be the people who read stories.

B and D. Television and clubs have nothing to do with reading of any kind.

C. People who dislike reading must dislike both prose and poetry. The prose-bound community thus would exclude the people who dislike reading in general.

6. A

The *quatrain* has a four-line verse structure. This poem is arranged in verses, or stanzas, of four lines each.

A. A *sestet* is a six-line verse.

B. An *octave* is an eight-line verse.

D. The *sonnet* is a fourteen-line poem.

7. A

The speaker offers advice to future poets. The fact that he supposes that poets may benefit from his suggestions indicates that he feels some optimism about the future of poetry.

B. The first four stanzas do seem pessimistic, but then the tone changes.

C. The speaker does seem ambivalent when he states that he does not know about the future of poetry (line 13). However, from line 17 on, he speaks with certainly, not ambivalence.

D. The mention of bombs in the third stanza might suggest terror, but the tone of the words is detached. There is no intensity of feeling in lines 9 to 12.

8. D

Blank verse has a regular rhythm, but no rhyme. Even though we may not be certain about the meaning, we know that it refers to verse that does not rhyme because in the context of the poem, it is placed in opposition to verse that does rhyme (line 18).

A. Verse is either blank or rhyming (line 18). If it is blank, then it does not rhyme.

B. The point of line 18 is *rhyme*, not rhythm.

C. Blank can suggest confusing or confused—*He gave a blank look*. However, the context limits the meaning of blank to some form of verse.

Reading Two

from "Eye of the Moon"
Sarah Klassen

9. A

Nana's eye surgery happened before the places Julia had applied to could call her (which makes **B** incorrect). Her parents let her choose whether or not she wanted to look after Nana, but they would pay her if she did.

C. Her friends have jobs, but that doesn't mean they took all the jobs.

D. Her father did say that she has the rest of her life to work, but Julia had planned to get a job anyway.

10. D

In paragraph 3, Julia's father's attitude is explained — he is not direct with her and feels awkward dealing with "an adolescent in the volatile process of becoming a woman."

A and B are incorrect because they both apply to the mother, not the father, and there is no indication of **C** in the passage. Julia herself is happy to exercise more, not because her father has said anything about it.

11. B

Onomatopoeia is a word that represents a sound, as in the *buzz* of flies. Other examples are *hiss* or *creak*.

A. Alliteration is the repetition of initial consonant sounds as in *four ferocious felines*.

C. Irony exists when words are intended to express something opposite or different to their literal meaning or when the opposite of what one expects to happen occurs.

D. Symbolism is when a concrete object represents an abstract idea; for example, a dove can represent peace.

12. D

A metaphor is a comparison between two unlike things, or the transfer of the ideas around one object on to another. Here, Nana's state of mind is compared with the game of marbles. That she has all her marbles means that she still has her whole mind.

B. propaganda is information that is spread for the purpose of promoting a cause.

13. A

This is a narrative passage because it tells a story. It does not attempt to persuade the reader (**C**) or argue a point (**D**).

B. Satirical writing makes fun of human follies or vices.

14. B

To balk to is to stop or to refuse. This line shows that Julia is not quite so fond of her other grandmother.

15. C

Being able to see more plays is the only response that is not a benefit. Julia earns money (**A**), gets in shape from jogging

(**B**) and has free time in between the applications (**D**).

16. A

In paragraph 19, Nana assumes that Julia has come for a visit, not realizing she's just there to do her job, so Nana is surprised when Julia leaves.

17. D

Paragraph 22 — "...the days of summer vacation were running past without anything happening. That was the summer I first began reflecting on time..." Neither **A** nor **B** are causes for reflection, and **C** is incorrect.

18. A

A simile is a comparison using *like* or *as*, "like a china doll's," hence **A** is correct. Personification is when human qualities are given to an inanimate object. In this case, a china doll does have eyelids, so it is not an example of personification. "The blackboards watched the students enter the classroom" is an example of personification.

19. A

"Hardy" best describes Nana. She is described as being a "tough bird" who takes care of herself for the most part. She is not squeamish **B** about her eye drops, she simply can't get the hang of doing them herself. There is no evidence to support **C** or **D**.

Reading Three

"Scientists Solve 2,000-Year-Old-Mystery"
Joseph Brean

20. A

The article explains how geckos' feet stick to surfaces. Everything in the article is about the gecko's remarkable ability.

B. The article describes some applications. It does not encourage people to think of new ways.

C. The article does teach, but only about geckos, not about lizards in general.

D. Applications of gecko research are mentioned only as interesting asides. In fact, there are no glues ready to be marketed.

21. C

Dr. Kellar Autumn solved the mystery.

A. There is no one named Lewis Clark. Dr. Autumn works at Lewis & Clark College.

B. Joseph Brean wrote the article.

D. Aristotle first marveled at geckos. (And you will recall that he lived about 2 500 years ago.)

22. A

Paragraph 4 explains that an electrical bond is what allows geckos' feet to stick to surfaces.

B, C, and **D**—glue, a water bond, and a chemical reaction have been suggested at different times as possible explanations. These ideas have been shown to be wrong.

23. C

Dr. Autumn marvelled about the movie because it was true to biology. The part he marvelled at was the gecko-like hairs that let the character climb walls. The movie device is fanciful, but it does echo Dr. Autumn's real discovery.

A. Dr. Autumn saw the movie on a flight. Nothing more is said about the flight or its possible effect on the scientist's judgement.

B. The genetically modified spider has no connection to the gecko. It is also the least true to biology.

D. *In a biological way* means *real*. But gecko-like hairs on a human hand are most probably impossible. The movie device is *realistic* (looks plausible and has some connection to reality) but it is not *real*.

24. A

This question requires a careful reading of paragraph 11 to identify the correct response. The hairs on spiders' legs might have the same purpose as the hairs on geckos' feet. If so, then spiders and geckos might be examples of the independent development of similar traits.

B. Destruction of the environment is not mentioned at all. It has nothing to do with either spiders or geckos.

C. It is possible that the evolution of the two animals converges; it does not diverge.

D. The structures are not convergent, they are similar. It is the evolution that is (possibly) convergent.

25. C

Paragraph 18 describes how the foot does not stick if its angle against a surface is greater than 30 degrees.

A. The *push*, mentioned in paragraph 19, makes the foot stick.

B. The foot does pop off, but only after it is angled correctly.

D. The very precise forces needed to make the foot stick are described in paragraph 19.

26. D

Military agencies generally perform research in the hope that the results have military applications.

A. Gecko-gloves for football players are mentioned in the article. However, there is no reason to connect football with a defense agency.

B. This scientist obviously did not vow to work in secret. He has published his findings.

C. A gecko-footed robot for exploring Mars is mentioned briefly, but there is no reason to connect Mars with a defense agency.

27. C

Jargon is specialized language of a particular group or the technical terminology of a specific subject.

A. False reasoning is when there are faults or errors in an argument, so that any conclusion drawn is not a logical one.

B and **D.** These words are neither viewpoints nor definitions.

28. B

Metaphor. The writer is comparing the bond that holds the feet to the wall to glue.

Reading Four

World Cup 1998
Kate Braid

29. C

There are many words in the poem that focus the reader on the passion of the game — "desperately" "fierce competition," "purest pleasure," "embrace and cry," and "love." Some of the other aspects (**A**, **B** and **D**) are mentioned in the poem, but are not the main focus.

30. A

A stereotype is when a person is portrayed as conforming to a set image, for example "Women are emotional," or "Teenagers are terrible." In the beginning of this poem, men are shown as the stereotypical strong athletes, but at the end of the poem, this stereotype is broken when they embrace and cry.

There is no support in the poem for **B**, **C**, or **D**.

31. D

Theme is the universal idea that is the focus of the poem. A theme is contained in a literary work such as a poem, but it also applies to life and to readers' experiences. Therefore **A** and **B** are incorrect as they are too specific. **C** is a fine theme statement, but it is not the theme of this poem. The correct answer is **D**, because the speaker shows how passionate the players are and how emotional they become. This idea applies not only to the soccer players, but to anyone who has ever been passionate about something.

32. A

The speaker intends the reader to see soccer as an art form, where the players' bodies leap or fly through the air just as beautiful ballet dancers do. **B** is incorrect as there is not mention of practice. **C** is incorrect because the speaker compares the athlete to the dancer, not the dancer to the athlete. Although **D** may be true, the choreography of the team is not mentioned in the poem.

33. B

"France vs. Norway, Brazil vs. Spain" shows that the languages spoken by the teams are different. "their bodies speak an old familiar language" shows that what they do physically and without thinking is the same regardless of where they are from. Thus **B** is the correct response.

34. B

Metaphor. A metaphor is a comparison between two unlike things, or the transfer of the ideas around one object on to another. Here, the soccer ball is compared with a firefly, because fireflies are quick and flash around a field.

B Simile must use "like" or "as" to compare, such as if the poet had written "The soccer ball is like a firefly."

C An oxymoron is the use of contradictory words for a special effect.

D Conflict is an element of fiction where one side opposes another (for example, person vs. person, person vs. nature).

35. C

The players are in "fierce competition" for the symbol, so it follows that the thing that they are in competition for is victory and there are several references in the poem to the desire to win. **B**, Power is close, but victory is a more accurate description.

ANSWERS AND SOLUTIONS –
PRACTICE EXAMINATION 3

1. B	8. A	15. B	22. B	29. B
2. A	9. B	16. D	23. A	30. A
3. D	10. C	17. B	24. C	31. C
4. C	11. D	18. D	25. A	32. B
5. B	12. B	19. B	26. A	33. C
6. A	13. C	20. B	27. B	
7. B	14. D	21. D	28. D	

Reading One

"You Had Two Girls"
Duncan Campbell Scott

1. B

The best response fully describes what happens: a logjam becomes unstuck, but kills a logger and a woman. The other responses are true but limited.

A. A man and a woman do drown on the river.

C. The speaker does address Baptiste.

D. Loggers did lead a dangerous life.

2. A

The repetition of sounds emphasizes that the logs are tightly stuck. The words not only rhyme, they have similar connotations. The repetition of meaning and sound emphasizes that the logs were stuck tight.

B. The logs were not making any sound. They were not moving.

C. Frustration is more evident in the following words: "The Devil had clinched them below."

D. The repetition includes one example of internal rhyme. All the other rhymes are end rhymes. Also, any poetic technique is meant to emphasize meaning, not to emphasize the technique itself.

3. D

The lightness of Dufour's song emphasizes his skill and daring, and his courage in the face of danger. When the whole jam roars free, he cannot make it to the shore, so without hesitation, he leaps forward, riding a log out ahead of the rush. His coolness and his confident boasting (he "tossed us a song") as he kept his balance ("floated along") on a bucking log contrasts with the tragedy of his drowning an instant later as he is thrown into the water and crushed.

A. The *grinding* "like a wolf's jaws" as the jam breaks has ended. Now that the logs are moving, they are *roaring*.

B. The men cheer for Dufour's daring and skill, and for his hair's-breadth escape from the logs. The cheers are part of the setup for the tragic contrast that follows.

C. The woman is not yet in the canoe. She takes to the water when she sees Dufour fall back.

4. C

The girl dared to paddle straight into the crush of logs. It is not clear whether she meant to try to save Dufour or if she meant to follow him no matter what (line 64 suggests the second possibility). Either way, *brave* is the best word to describe her.

A. *Hysterical* implies a loss of control. Her actions are too purposeful for hysteria.

B. *Carelessness* suggests disregard for consequences. She knows what is at stake and acts anyway.

D. Her actions are quick and determined. She shows no sign of fear.

5. B

The quick, sharp sound of the word "cracked" emphasizes the ease with which the heavy logs snap her canoe—we know how quickly and completely a shell cracks.

A. The fact that she drowns is enough to imply that she should not have followed Dufour into the water. The vivid image of a cracking shell serves the purpose that is already described in alternative **B**.

C. Shells do crack easily, but there is no shell in the scene, only the fragile canoe. The shell is mentioned for the sake of the simile.

D. No one would know how to how to paddle a canoe "in that rush of hell."

6. A

In lines 11 to 21, "we" free the logs. In line 29, "I" and ten other loggers scramble ashore as the logs move. It must be one of the loggers who is breaking the news to Baptiste.

B. The narrator names Virginie, so it cannot be Virginie.

C. The father is Baptiste.

D. Dufour is dead.

7. B

Of course the man knows the names of both sisters. But at the beginning of the poem, after naming Virginie he breaks off without naming her sister because Baptiste guesses and is about to rush away. At the end, Baptiste does rush off, and the narrator is left to repeat his words. Only now he ends dramatically: "What God calls the other / Is not known to me." He is not ignorant of the name she went by before her death. Her name is held back to emphasize the drama and the tragedy.

A. Since we know nothing of Virginie but her name, her degree of courage has nothing to do with the poem.

C. It is possible that the logger happened to know the name of only one of Baptiste's daughters. However, there is no evidence of that, and the line 71 makes it clear that it is the fact of her death that determines how he speaks of her.

D. Given the "rush of hell" that could toss a tree trunk 30 feet, it did not matter if she could swim. And again, line 71 is the dramatic point of the poem.

Reading Two

from *Eve's Ransom*
George Gissing

8. A

Note the statement "her face made him welcome," (paragraph 5). This suggests that Hilliard and his sister-in-law have a comfortable relationship.

B. She is uncertain what Hilliard will think of her marrying. She is embarrassed (paragraph 5), and she turns away while speaking about it (paragraph 37). Also they usually see each other only once a month (paragraph 9). It seems that they were not intimate.

C and D. When she is afraid of offending Hilliard (paragraph 16), he laughs and says, "Not likely. I can take a good deal from you." This is clear evidence that their relationship is not distant or tense.

9. B

Maurice Hilliard tells Mrs. Hilliard that he has received a cheque that covers a debt owed his father by Dengate. We can safely infer that the money is the reason that he seems a different man. (Remember the information in the footnote: it was a large amount of money.)

A. The money that is owed to the father is paid to the son, and the son shares it with his sister-in-law. We may infer that the father is dead and his son and daughter-in-law are his only living relatives and have inherited the right to the money. In this sense, Hilliard is paid the money that is owed to him. However, because *the money is also owed to his sister-in-law*, this answer is incomplete.

C. The money—not 436 pounds but a cheque for that sum—was paid to the son, not to the father. Since the son then treats the money as his own, it seems the father must be dead. (The son is shown to be a decent man. There is not reason to believe he is stealing from his father. He must have inherited the right to the money.)

D. In paragraph 26, Hilliard tosses the cheque into the air with boyish glee. This shows that the cheque is the cause of his high spirits. The invitation is not the cause.

10. C

"I'm not quite sure I understand the reptile" (paragraph 25). Hilliard says that Dengate is a reptile. This direct statement is a metaphor comparing Dengate's character with the qualities of a reptile.

A. The same comparison, made with the words *like* or *as*, would be a *simile*.

B. Depending on how bad Dengate really is, the metaphor might also be *hyperbole*, an exaggeration for effect. (Of course, Dengate might actually fit the description, so this response is not correct.)

D. *Personification* attributes, or gives, human qualities to abstractions or to objects—and sometimes to animals. However, this figure of speech ascribes animal qualities to a Dengate, a human being.

11. D

The answer might seem obvious—and perhaps it is. " 'I told him he was a scoundrel, and he began by threatening to thrash me. I'm very glad he didn't try. It was in the train, and *I know very well I should have strangled him*. It would have been awkward, you know' " (paragraph 28)

The only problem here is that a careful reader will notice that Hilliard is not serious. His tone gives him away. It was in the train (meaning there were witnesses) and "it would have been awkward, you know" (awkward being one way of describing the consequences of murder). Then his sister-in-law cries, "Oh, Maurice, how can you——?" (*Can*, not *could*. She is reacting to his jesting words and his tone.) However, this is still the only possible answer, even though Hilliard does not mean what he says.

A and **B**—Although Hilliard is threatened, he makes Dengate pay up. He is confident enough to stand his ground and make Dengate back down.

C. It is true that dead men write no cheques. However, the lack of the cheque would have been the least of Hilliard's worries if he had strangled Dengate.

12. B

The news that she tells Maurice is that she intends to marry Ezra Marr.

A. She does not even hear about the money until Hilliard has accepted the invitation and is actually in her house.

C. *Eloping* is running away to be married. Mrs. Hilliard would not ask for Hilliard's approval if she meant to elope.

D. Yes, she has some news. But the news is about her intended marriage. This response is included in response B.

13. C

Mrs. Hilliard is reluctant to accept half the money because Hilliard has already done so much for her, but she is able to refuse because "I sha'n't want it" (paragraph 31). *I shall not want it*—although she may be short of money now, she will not be in the future. The reason, which Hilliard immediately guesses, is that she is getting remarried. She might not like to take more from Hilliard, but she is able to refuse because she will soon be married.

A. Although he has done so much for her, this is not the main reason she refuses. She actually refuses because her impending marriage makes it possible for her to refuse.

B. She already has his affections. The whole passage shows that they are on affectionate terms.

D. Since Hilliard, in the last line, insists that half of the money is hers, he must really intend to give it to her.

14. D

In this context, *ground* means reason. Hilliard thinks about her marriage and realizes that his objections are not sensible. The marriage is a good idea and he has no reason to object to it.

A. It is not that he cannot resist her approach. Instead, he agrees with her.

B. Losing ground would mean that he is overwhelmed or out-argued. However, after he hears her news, his first thinks about, and then approves her decision.

C. He does feel objections at first. However, he does not stand his ground, or feel the need to stand his ground. Instead, he thinks the idea through and dismisses his objections.

Reading Three

"Schools Use Daily Gym Class In Battle
With Child Obesity"
Heather Sokoloff

15. B

The title of the article explains that schools
use gym classes to battle obesity. Schools
can require students to attend more phys. ed.
classes, which will make them more active.

A According to the article, some schools are
trying to lessen competition.

C. Some schools may need to make better
use of space, but this is not the reason for
having more phys. ed. classes.

D. The video games are not the reason for
the additional classes. The obesity that
can come of too much inactivity is the
reason.

16. D

In the quotation in paragraph 11, Dueck
explains that cutting kids from teams is
devastating because they aren't given the
chance to become great athletes. **A** is
incorrect. **B** and **C** may be true in some
cases, but are not reasons given in the
article.

17. B

The use of these words emphasize that the
writer thinks that the phys. ed. requirements
are not strong enough. Notice the difference
between "There are three classes a week"
and "There are ONLY three classes a week."
Bias is when a writer influences the reader
to have the same opinion has her/him. Bias
can be weak, moderate or strong. When
there is bias present, we can say the article is
biased or the writer is biased. **D** is the
writer's opinion. The question asks what we
learn about the article, not about the system
in Ontario.

18. D

D is the correct answer. See paragraph 15.

Reading Four

"When to Her Lute Corinna Sings"
Thomas Campion

19. B

Corinna's music stirs deep emotions in the
poet: "And as her lute doth live or die, / Led
by her passion, so must I" (lines 7–8). The
idea can be extended to music and people in
general.

A. *Challenge* has nothing to do with
Corinna's audience. In line 4, the word is
used as a metaphor: an echo responds to a
voice as someone might respond to a
challenge. When Corinna sings her words
give life to the strings and they echo her
voice.

(Campion was an Elizabethan, a
contemporary of Shakespeare.
The Elizabethans loved complex figures
of speech.)

C. The strings do not literally break, as
though the instrument were in disrepair.
They break metaphorically, like a heart.

D. Life and death are mentioned in line 7,
but each is matched metaphorically to a
different kind of song. In lines 9 and 10,
life is matched with songs of pleasure. In
lines 11 and 12, death is matched with
songs of sorrow.

20. B

Corinna's singing and playing ("When to her lute Corinna sings") give life to the lute strings. The strings are leaden without her playing. In other words, she plays beautifully.

A. The strings are not dying, they are leaden.

C. The poem is all about music. It has nothing to do with appearance, with the look of a thing.

D. The strings do echo her voice, but not in line 2.

21. D

Corinna's lute *lives and dies*. This is an example of *personification*, or the attribution of human characteristics to inanimate objects.

A. An *oxymoron* is the use of contradictory words for special effect. *They responded with a deafening silence.* Notice that the contradiction is only on the surface. *Deafening silence* makes perfect sense.

B. A *metaphor* is the comparing of two unlike things by making a literal statement that is not meant to be taken literally. *A hawk-faced soldier stood guard.*

C. *Hyperbole* is exaggeration used for rhetorical effect. *An hour of her singing was pure torture.*

22. B

Since the poem is already full of images of life and death, the best response is to say that his mind comes to life like the world coming to life in spring. Spring's new life follows winter's death.

A. *Thoughts spring up* could be a metaphor for the appearance of new thoughts. However, the whole stanza is developing the metaphor of the lute living and dying. Response B fits better.

C. A spring of water can be metaphor for life, so *drinking from a spring* would fit the rest of the stanza. However, response A contains a fuller metaphor because it contains an unspoken contrasting image of winter.

D. *Bouncing like a spring* does not fit at all. The image is slightly ridiculous when compared with other images in the poem.

23. A

How can we tell a shift takes place from the first to the second stanzas? Although the second stanza opens with a reference to the lute, as did the first stanza, the line that follows contains the clue. The pronoun "I" at the end of the line indicates that the speaker has shifted his thoughts from their focus on Corinna's singing to a new focus on the effect that Corinna has on himself (lines 8–10).

B. Corinna's heart is not mentioned at all. She may feel nothing when she sings—or she may feel a lot. She sings of happiness and sorrow, but there is not a word to say what she feels.

C. The shift from Corinna's singing to her speaking is found at the end of the second stanza, not in the change between the two stanzas.

D. Although the first person "I" is used only in the second stanza, its presence is implied in the first by the fact that the poet is speaking throughout the poem.

24. C

"But if she does of sorrow speak," (line 11). When Corinna speaks, she speaks of sorrow.

A and **D.** These responses simply do not fit.

B. Unhappiness is a synonym for sorrow. However, always choose the clearest answer. Since sorrow is actually named in the poem (line 11), it is the best answer.

25. A

The rhyme scheme is *aabbcc,* and so on. Each pair of lines rhymes. The poem is written in *rhyming couplets.*

B. *Free verse* does not have a regular rhythm, or meter, nor does it rhyme.

C. *Blank verse* has a regular rhythm, or meter, but it does not rhyme.

D. *Quatrains* are four-line stanzas. This poem is arranged in six-line stanzas.

Reading Five

"Where the Reids Lived"
Mary Bowen

26. A

The writer states she doesn't see Cathedral mountain as large and strong the way the artist did. She has different memories, associations, and experiences with both Cathedral mountain and the house, so we say she has a different point of view (also referred to as viewpoint — how we see things).

B. There is no indication in the text that she is either more critical or less critical in adulthood than she was as a child.

C and D. Neither response has any basis in the text. We can assume she goes to the gallery because she does appreciate and understand art.

27. B

The writer describes how she wanted to catch a glimpse of the artist's yard and how she wanted to see "what a real artist looked like." She was intrigued by him.

A. and **D.** She didn't think he was intimidating or aloof, because she didn't know anything about him. There is some suggestion that her mother intimidated her a little, but the artist was not intimidating.

C. The artist is talented, but the question asks what the writer as a young girl thought about him. At that point in her life, she mostly thought he was intriguing. It is not until she is older that she becomes familiar with his work.

28. D

Imagery is an appeal to the senses — sight, hearing, touch, taste and smell — to create a vivid description. The writer uses many sensory descriptions in this paragraph such as "feel the warm draft" and "smell the wet wool mittens."

A. There are not various viewpoints (how we see things) in this paragraph. She describes the house from her point of view only, so there are not many examples.

B. A stereotype is an oversimplified character. This paragraph is not about character.

C. Foreshadowing is a plot device where a writer gives subtle hints about what will happen later in the story.

29. B

Tone is a writer's attitude toward her subject (what she is writing about). Nostalgia is a sentimental look at the past. This most accurately describes the tone of this piece.

A, amused, and **C**, sympathetic, are inaccurate, and **D**, melodramatic, is too strong.

30. A

A metaphor takes the ideas around one object and transfers them to another and thus compares the two. The writer compares the feeling of suddenly being in the past when she looks at the painting of her house to being in a time machine. It serves to show how quickly her mind can move to a different time in her life.

B. and **C.** are true in that the past is important and she is able to recall the details of her old house, but have nothing to do with the time machine metaphor.

D. The time machine metaphor helps divide the past and present, but the main purpose is not to create a contrast between her old house and the art gallery.

31. C

Style refers to the manner of writing, or the way a person writes. In this piece, the writer works to capture and convey her feelings and memories, thus her style is emotive.

A. The writer talks about things from the past, but she does not write in an old or antiquated style.

B. An elevated style would contain complex grammatical structures and more difficult vocabulary.

C. The writer's style is not formal.

Connections

32. B

Both the speaker in the poem and the writer in the personal essay are transported by the art: the speaker's feelings follow Corinna's lute, and the writer's imagination is taken back to her childhood. There is no evidence to support **A** or **C**. There is some indication that the writer is paying close attention (**D**), but there is no mention of how closely the poem's speaker is listening, nor is there evidence in either piece that a person must pay close attention to appreciate the art.

33. C

The speaker in the poem clearly enjoys the music, and says "My thoughts enjoy a sudden spring." In the same way, the writer obviously enjoys the paintings and says "Oh, but I am enjoying myself!" There is some evidence that the speaker feels sad or depressed (**C**) at one point, but the writer does not.

APPENDIX 1

Tips for Studying

Tests and Papers

1. Find a quiet, well-lit location where you are not likely to be disturbed by the telephone or by other people. This place could be anywhere you feel most comfortable, including your own home, a coffee shop or the library.

2. Start with class notes. Your teacher chooses to emphasize certain issues in class, so go through his or her notes carefully. Can you determine what material your teacher emphasized? What evidence did the teacher take from the texts you read in class? Although you should have read all of the class material by the time tests and essays roll around, you may not have enough time to re-read all of these works over again. Instead, focusing on the passages that were underscored by your instructor will help you provide the appropriate evidence for the argument you are advancing.

3. Consider starting or joining a study group. You may want to call up a friend who is in your class, or someone you think cares as much as you do about their performance in the class. Each person tends to have their individual strengths and can help others in that area, and you may mutually benefit from responding to each others' questions. As well, explaining an answer in your own words to someone with your own level of understanding can help you understand your own thoughts about a question. Your study buddy might not understand something that you thought was obvious. Explaining your answer to this person can help you write a more complete answer for your teacher when it comes time to finish a test.

    To avoid the temptation of talking about other, more 'interesting', topics than your class material, you may want to schedule yourselves a break after an hour of concentrated work. You may also want to set yourself a goal of having studied a certain number of pages of course material before taking a break. If you get up for a walk after having worked hard, you will feel like you deserved the break, and may well find yourselves talking about a question from your study notes, even as you take a break.

4. Find out as much information about the exam as you can ahead of time. Ask your teacher about the format and content. Will the test consist of an essay question, a short answer, multiple choice, or some combination of these? Which concepts from the course material will be emphasized? You might also want to ask your teacher for copies of old exams. The content of the present exam will probably differ from previous exams, but you get a sense of the kind of questions your instructor tends to ask. Reading an old exam will help you get a feel for the way your teacher words questions, the way he or she frames them. The specific questions may change over the years, but you may notice that your instructor approaches a particular text through questions about characterization. He or she may approach another through questions about setting. Having a thorough knowledge about the issues that are associated with each of these approaches can help you produce a smart response to the question on the actual exam.

5. Have you ever created a *crib* sheet? Condense the most important information onto a small piece of paper. As you know, you cannot take this paper with you into the exam room. Although you may be tempted to cheat, the risks you take of getting caught, failing the exam and perhaps the entire course, are certainly not worth it. From tests that you've successfully passed as a result of your own hard work, you know the relief and satisfaction you feel when you leave an exam room after having tried your very best.

We call crib sheets "mnemonic" devices because they help us to remember information that would otherwise be a scrambled mess in our memories. You will want to make the crib sheet as easy to visualize as possible. If you cannot picture it in your mind when it is time to answer the questions on the exam, your crib sheet is not very much use to you. Can you think of single words, or short phrases that can summarize points your teacher made? What sequence is formed by their first letters if you line them up one on top of the other? Do these first letters form another word? Can you make them all begin with the same letter (the five E's of excellence, for example). Can you more easily visualize these important words if you underline them with another colour ink, or highlight them with a highlighter? Putting all of this creative effort into your crib sheet may seem like a waste of time at first. However, it will only be a waste of time if you forget that you are creating a small document to help trigger your memory when you need this information during the exam. Once you get inside the test room and get your exam paper, you can re-create the crib sheet from memory onto the back of a test page to help you while you take the exam.

This outline will help you stay focused while writing your exam responses. Since most exams take place within time frames that never seem to be enough to write everything the teacher wants you to say, it is wise to stay as focused as possible, addressing only the question specified by the exam.

Test Time
1. **Flip through the entire exam to find the format of the exam.** Together with finding the kind of questions your teacher is asking, you can also find the point value your teacher assigned each section. Which sections are worth the most? These sections should receive the most of your time. Divide the total amount of exam-writing time among the sections of the test. How much time should you spend on each section based on the points assigned to those sections?

2. **Do the easy questions first.** When you start with a difficult question, it is easy to get bogged down and not leave enough time to finish other questions, even ones you know really well. You don't want to lose points on questions to which you know the answers, just because you ran out of time. As well, if you begin with the questions that you know the best, you may feel more confident in tackling the ones that are more difficult for you. Just make sure that you leave yourself enough time to work through the difficult questions. Since you have left them to the end of the exam you may run out of time to give your best effort to the question. Remember that the teacher cannot give grades for information that you do not include in the test.

3. **Read the directions carefully.** Take note of verbs such as, such as "take note," "compare," "discuss." Although a discussion may seem less formal than a comparison, in a test situation your responses should be written in formal language. They should be constructed with a thesis sentence. They should each have an introduction, body and conclusion, as you will have discussed in your class. While the language of your response should be clear instead of unnecessarily complex, formal writing in an exam situation should avoid language that is too casual such as slang. When composing your response, be certain that your answer addresses the question. Although your answer may be correct, if it is not the answer that responds to the question, your teacher will regretfully not be able to offer your answer any of the marks it may otherwise deserve.

4. **Answer every question.** Although you might have tried to study everything as thoroughly as possible, a test question may sometimes catch you by surprise. Instead of not answering the question at all, you should answer as much of the question as you can. Your teacher cannot give the same grade that he would for a finished answer, but he or she can give some grades for the information you did demonstrate that you knew. These few percentage points can sometimes lift your mark from the top of one letter grade into the next.

5. **If possible, leave some time at the end of the exam to go over your answers.** Giving your answers one final appraisal before turning them in, can help you clean up answers, by including words you may have omitted in your haste to get the answer down. You may also realize upon a second reading that something you thought was well-expressed, actually might be stronger if you re-worded it. If you leave yourself time near the end of the exam, you can add some polish to an answer that will make it sparkle, instead of remaining dull with errors. The pride and care that you take in your own work shines through answers that have been edited for grammatical mistakes and typos. This care translates into stronger results for you.

Reading a Returned Exam

1. Don't first compare answers and grades with your friends in the same class. Instead of using the instructor's comments to understand the class material on a deeper level, your focus shifts to the more superficial level of the grades your friends may be receiving. At some point you may wish to share your results with your classmates, but you will miss a great opportunity to learn from the exam if you compare these results too soon.

2. When you receive your exam, you try to find a quiet, comfortable place to read through your work and the teacher's comments. If the grade you received is much lower than the one you expected for this work, take a moment to understand your teacher's response. It's possible that your teacher could make a mistake, since teacher's are fallible too. But although some grades may make you feel angry, or hurt, if you nonetheless try to learn from the exchange between your answer & your teacher's, you may be able to avoid making a similar mistake in the future. If after considering the teacher's grade you are not able to understand how he or she arrived at their response, you could make an appointment to see your instructor in the next day or two. A few nights' sleep may help you feel more calm about your evaluation. If

you approach your meeting with your teacher with a sincerely open attitude to learn, your instructor will no doubt be happy to assist you, or recommend someone else who could.

3. The exam is over. You have no intention of attempting that same exam ever again. However, you may find it useful to sketch an outline for an answer that was weak on your exam. This exercise needn't take much time and if you ever encounter a similar question on a later, more comprehensive examination, you will have learnt from your initial response and will know a more sound approach.

Papers

1. Try to start your work the same day you get the assignment, and then set your goal of always staying ahead of the paper's deadline instead of running slightly behind it. At this first stage you won't be writing yet but you could begin your initial thinking about the topic, brainstorming some approaches, discussing your ideas with a teacher at an appointment, and making an initial search through the library's database for resources. You could ask the librarian to help you for a few minutes as well. No one could make your life easier in a library than the librarian, of course, since he or she will both know the collection of books and journals as well as the best ways to access this collection.

2. Make sure your paper is completed at least two to three days before it is due. This gives you a chance to put it down and get some perspective. Come back to your paper a day or so before it is due and re-read it. Chances are you will find sentences you want to re-write, paragraphs you'd like to make stronger, or maybe just some grammatical errors you need to correct. In any case, your paper will be that much better than if you'd just rushed it in as soon as you were finished writing.

APPENDIX 2

Literary Terms and Devices

Students should be familiar with the following terms and devices in literature.

Alliteration	Jargon	Sonnet
Bias	Metaphor	Stereotypes
Character	Mood	Stock/stereotypical character
Climax	Onomatopoeia	Style
Conflict	Pace	Symbolism
False reasoning	Parody	Theme
Foreshadowing	Plot	Tone
Forum	Propaganda	Viewpomts
Genre	Satire	
Imagery	Setting	
Irony	Simile	

APPENDIX 3

Types FSA Reading Passages

Types of reading passages used in the Foundations Skills Assessment include the following:

- plays
- poetry
- novels
- short fiction
- essays (formal or informal style)
- discontinuous texts (e.g., tables, charts, graphs, web pages)
- non-fiction prose (diaries, journals, letters, newspaper columns)

CREDITS

Every effort has been made to provide proper acknowledgment of the original source and to comply with copyright law. However, some attempts to establish original copyright ownership may have been unsuccessful. If copyright ownership can be identified, please notify Castle Rock Research Corp so that appropriate corrective action can be taken.

Practice Examinataion 1

Excerpt from *Emma*, by Jane Austin

Stars by Marjorie Pickthall

Closet of the Future Picks Out Clothes, Hans Greimel, The National Post, September 10, 2002

Table: *Percentage of Internet users, aged 15 and over, by selected types of Internet activity, Canada and province, 2000*, from Statistics Canada, General Social Survey, Cycle 14

Pantoum for a Mother in Nunavut, Claire Battershill

Practice Examination 2

On the Future of Poetry, Henry Austin Dobson

Eye of the Moon, Sarah Klassen, first published in The Antigonish Review, no. 133, Spring 2003

Scientists solve 2,000-year-old mystery of geckos' glue, Joseph Brean, published in the National Post, August 27, 2002

World Cup 1998, Kate Braid, The Canadian Journal of Poetry and Critical Writing (Vol. 26, Issue 1, Summer 2003)

Practice Examination 3

You Had Two Girls, Duncan Campbell Scott

Excerpt from *Eve's Ransom*, George Gissing

Schools use daily gym class in battle with child obesity, Heather Sokoloff, The National Post

When to Her Lute Corinna Sings, Thomas Campion

Where the Reids Lived, Mary Bowen, The National Post, March 22, 2004

ORDERING INFORMATION

INDIVIDUAL ORDERS	SCHOOL ORDERS
ORDER ONLINE at www.castlerockresearch.com or contact Castle Rock Research BC Toll-free: 1.866.882.8246 Fax: 250.868.9146	Schools and school jurisdictions are eligible for our **educational discount** rate. Contact Castle Rock Research BC for more information.

THE KEY Study Guides are specifically designed to assist students in preparing for unit tests, final exams, and provincial examinations.

KEY Study Guides – $29.95 each plus G.S.T.

SENIOR HIGH		JUNIOR HIGH	ELEMENTARY
Biology 12 Chemistry 12 English 12 Geography 12 History 12 Physics 12 Principles of Math 12	Biology 11 Chemistry 11 English 11 Physics 11 Principles of Math 11 English 10 Principles of Math 10 Science 10	Language Arts 9 Math 9 Language Arts 7 Math 7	Math 6 Language Arts 4 Math 4

Student Notes and Problems (SNAP) Workbooks contain complete explanations of curriculum concepts, examples, and exercise questions.

SNAP Workbooks – $29.95 each plus G.S.T.

SENIOR HIGH		JUNIOR HIGH	ELEMENTARY
Principles of Math 12 Physics 12	Principles of Math 11 Physics 11 Principles of Math 10	Science 9 Math 9 Math 8 Math 7	Math 6 Math 5 Math 4 Math 3

For students in the following courses, we have available the following corresponding resources which are correlated to the B.C. curriculum.

B.C. COURSE NAME	CORRESPONDING RESOURCE
Applications of Math 12	*THE KEY* – Math 30 Applied
Applications of Math 12	**SNAP** – Math 30 Applied
Applications of Math 11	**SNAP** – Math 20 Applied
Applications of Math 10	**SNAP** – Math 10 Applied
Calculus 12	**SNAP** – Math 31

**Visit our website for a "tour" of resource content and features,
or order online at
www.castlerockresearch.com**

#4 – 1905 Evergreen Court
Kelowna, BC Canada V1Y 9L4
e-mail: learnbc@castlerockresearch.com

Phone: 250.868.8384
Toll-free: 1.866.882.8246
Fax: 250.868.9146

ORDER FORM

ORDER ONLINE AT www.castlerockresearch.com

THE KEY	Price	Quantity	Total
Biology 12	$29.95		
Chemistry 12	$29.95		
English 12	$29.95		
Geography 12	$29.95		
History 12	$29.95		
Physics 12	$29.95		
Principles of Math 12	$29.95		
Biology 11	$29.95		
Chemistry 11	$29.95		
English 11	$29.95		
Physics 11	$29.95		
Principles of Math 11	$29.95		
English 10	$29.95		
Principles of Math 10	$29.95		
Science 10	$29.95		
Language Arts 9	$29.95		
Math 9	$29.95		
Language Arts 7	$29.95		
Math 7	$29.95		
Math 6	$29.95		
Language Arts 4	$29.95		
Math 4	$29.95		

SUBTOTAL 1

SNAP WORKBOOKS	Price	Quantity	Total
Physics 12	$29.95		
Principles of Math 12	$29.95		
Physics 11	$29.95		
Principles of Math 11	$29.95		
Principles of Math 10	$29.95		
Science 9	$29.95		
Math 9	$29.95		
Math 8	$29.95		
Math 7	$29.95		
Math 6	$29.95		
Math 5	$29.95		
Math 4	$29.95		
Math 3	$29.95		

SUBTOTAL 2

TOTAL COST OF BOOKS

SUBTOTAL 1	
SUBTOTAL 2	
SUBTOTAL 3	
COST SUBTOTAL	
SHIPPING AND HANDLING _Please call for current rates_	
G.S.T.	
ORDER TOTAL	

For students in the following courses, we recommend the corresponding Alberta resources which are highly correlated to the B.C. curriculum.

B.C. Course Name	Alberta Resource	Price	Quantity	Total
Applications of Math 12	THE KEY - Math 30 Applied	$29.95		
Applications of Math 12	SNAP - Math 30 Applied	$29.95		
Applications of Math 11	SNAP - Math 20 Applied	$29.95		
Applications of Math 10	SNAP - Math 10 Applied	$29.95		
Calculus 12	SNAP - Math 31	$29.95		

SUBTOTAL 3

Significant discounts for school orders. Prices subject to change.

Please complete the shipping and payment information.

Name: ____

Mailing Address: _____________________________________

City: _______________________ Postal Code: ___________

Telephone: _______________ School: _________________

VISA/MC Card Number: ____________ Expiry Date (mm/yy): _______

Name on Card: _______________________________________

ORDERING OPTIONS

On-line: www.castlerockresearch.com

Telephone: 250.868.8384 or 866.882.8246

Fax: 250.868.9146

E-mail: learnbc@castlerockresearch.com

Mail: #4 - 1905 Evergreen Court, Kelowna, BC V1Y 9L4

OR CONTACT YOUR DISTRICT REPRESENTATIVE

(Visit our website for the name of the representative in your area.)

www.castlerockresearch.com